"With love to my dear wife and daughter who have supported and helped me make this book a reality."

ABOUT THE AUTHOR

Michael Lia debut's his first sales reference book with Rebel Sales. Michael was born and raised in Sydney, Australia before moving to the United States to pursue his career. A successful tradesman and business owner for over thirty years, Michael shifted to a sales focus over a decade ago and has utilised his technical experience to build a highly successful career and outstanding reputation. The idea of capturing his ideas into the book Rebel Sales came from the many requests for guidance from his peers. In his personal time Michael enjoy's being in the outdoors and spending time with family.

BUILD SUCCESSFUL SALES IN THE REAL WORD

REBEL SALES

MICHAEL LIA

MINDSTIR MEDIA

Published by MindStir Media, LLC
45 Lafayette Rd | Suite 181| North Hampton, NH 03862 | USA
1.800.767.0531 | www.mindstirmedia.com

Printed in the United States of America.
ISBN-13: 978-1-961532-09-0

*"Let them call me rebel and welcome,
I feel no concern from it."*

– Thomas Paine, Political Activist, Theorist and Revolutionary

*I would sit in the middle of the pack (at best) and wonder why I
wasn't breaking through. It wasn't until I decided to stop following
all the rules that things truly changed.*
Well, now it's time to change things up and think for yourself.
It's your time to have that same breakthrough.

CONTENTS

CHAPTER 1

YOU HAVE TO START SOMEWHERE

Everything I write here comes from personal experience.

On your sales journey, you will hear from many so-called "experts" who have never personally ran a single sales call in their life. They will tell you how great it is and how easy it is to sell everything to customers. Frankly, they are full of hot air with zero substance, and even worse, zero experience. In my mind, it is impossible to take seriously a person who is pushing their perspective on sales training without actually having experienced it themselves firsthand.

How can they give you a guarantee on their training and its success rate if they have never actually executed their own training and techniques personally in the real world?

Experiencing the feeling of success and failure is crucial to learning and development. As you build your training and experience, be cautious of taking too much stock from the cut and paste, cookie-cutter training programs out there. If twenty other salespeople are peddling the same approach, how will you actually stand out and be uniquely successful? Ask yourself: How will mediocre mass-produced training and advice get you to the highest levels of success?

Hint: It won't.

There's a certain type of vulnerability that you will feel walking into a home in the very early stages of your career when you're still starting out and learning. I get that, I've been there. We've all been there. My aim is to try to help you streamline these actions and get more comfortable with your process quickly in order to find the truth within all the noise you have had rammed into your mind in the name of sales training.

CHAPTER 2

PREPARATION, CLARITY AND PERCEPTION

You must be completely clear in your mind in order to be able to have control of a sales call from start to close, without exception!

I don't care what is going on in your life. If you are wanting to take yourself to the highest level of consistent sales revenue that you desire, then you will need to resolve any issues that are clouding your mind, as this will alter your response when given a question from left field, such as when a customer abruptly questions your advice based on advice they have been given from a competing salesperson. With a clouded mind, you're not doing your job correctly and are wasting your customer's time, as well as your own! *Why do you think it is fair for you to waste another person's time?* You must learn how to control anything that's not related to your job at any particular moment in time. This is almost like flipping a switch inside your brain. This is something I learnt through sport, mostly when competing in motorsport. Given how extremely dangerous motorsport is at every second, it really can be a matter of life and death. If any thought other than driving that race car right on the limit was allowed to enter my thoughts, I would not be ready for the necessary offensive action I would need to make in order to avoid a major crash. Or, if not avoid the crash entirely, enter the crash in a way that I still have complete control over the outcome to ensure no one gets seriously hurt where possible. This may seem like an extreme example, but it is the most resounding way, based on my personal experience, to hammer home to you this important principle.

Remember: A clear and precise mind is needed when it's time to close for the win in the final stages of a race! A clear and precise mind closes sales when it is time to close for the revenue in the final stages!

A clear mind is one of the most crucial differences between being average and inconsistent, with mediocre sales revenue versus consistently producing the high sales revenue that you desire. It's not a magic trick at all. It is about discipline and knowing that when you start your day, your only focus is sales. When entering a sales call–unless you are trying to look like an amateur hack–**DO NOT** answer your cell phone! In fact, turn the mobile phone to silent (not vibrate). The phone can still be heard when vibrating in your pocket. Do this for **ALL** message alerts also. It's an amateur mistake to not take such a small step that can have a significant impact on the success of your sales call. Nothing is ruder to a customer than having the conversation interrupted even once by a completely unrelated phone call or message alert. You will not be able to give clear and confident responses to questions afterward, and at this point, no matter what comes out of your mouth, your body language will give it all away that you're not only distracted, but also embarrassed. If you were feeling confident and doing great it just went down the drain because of a cell phone. For you it's a lose-lose situation. Whether you answer the phone or not, you look rude to the customer and you lose. The simple fact is, you deserve to lose and be left empty-handed with no sale for not giving the customer the respect of silencing your cell phone so they can have your full attention and respect. Just think of how disappointed you will feel after learning how to clear your mind completely for the sales call only to have it all come crashing down over forgetting to silence your cell phone. Simple amateur mistake, significant impact to your success.

Remember: Professionals put their cell phone on silent (not vibrate) in board or company meetings so as not to disrespect management, so you should provide the same courtesy to the most important people: Your Customers!

Here is another very common mistake that everyone makes, no matter how experienced or inexperienced they are. It's just human nature.

As the age-old saying goes:

Do not judge a book by its cover!

We are all guilty of making assumptions about a person depending on how that person or their house looks. I know people that do this and have also seen it firsthand and am stunned every time. There are a lot of amateurs in sales that will look at a person's clothes or car to decide how much of their time the customer warrants. I have seen how this has failed on more than one occasion. This most commonly occurs in car sales.

Remember: Not everyone with money wants to wear a suit worth thousands of dollars or wear the latest sneakers or drive a flash car.

A lot of people with real money prefer to keep it invested, which is how they earned it in the first place. I have worked with customers ranging from Oscar winners to major sports athletes, and billionaires to those living in mobile homes in low-income communities. They all are equal in my mind and should be in yours when they choose to talk to you. And I can tell you one very important thing I learned over the years:

A dollar is a dollar, no matter who it comes from. It does not discriminate!

Don't judge a book by its cover and make the sale. Of course, you could be presenting different options based on what the customer is asking for and their needs. BUT, never let the way they look or where they live give you the perception or belief that you have the sole right to decide what you're going to offer them for sale without talking to them first. Some Ferrari drivers like wearing boardshorts - that's not a crime, is it? My advice is to never step on people on your way up, as life has a way of keeping you honest.

In short: Don't judge a book by its cover.

DON'T JUDGE A CUSTOMER BY THEIR COVER!

CHAPTER 3

AUTHENTIC PEOPLE GET AUTHENTIC RESULTS

Find your own individual style that works for you. Stop trying to be the same cookie-cutter solution that traditional sales training churns out. Authentic people attract authentic people and repeat sales success. It's that simple.

This is something I have communicated to everyone that has ever been trained by me, whether it be technical training or sales training. You will never get yourself to the next level by trying to impersonate another person. Authenticity costs nothing but will earn you respect and money. The person you try impersonating acts the way they do and says the things they say because it is what makes them comfortable. If you're not comfortable being yourself during a sales call, then you are also not confident which leads to doubting yourself and ultimately you lose control of the call.

This issue is one of the biggest barriers between being okay at your job and being the best at your job. Too often, what appears to be the easy road is taken. These quick and easy "steps" or "solutions" that promise success are often fleeting–just consider that if you and every other person in town are doing exactly the same thing, then what is your unique edge? What makes you stand out in the customers' mind? I will tell you. ABSOLUTELY NOTHING. Authenticity leads to trust and success, while disingenuous behavior easily tarnishes your position and leads to distrust.

You are being led down a road by your peers at work who are never giving the whole truth to the questions you are asking.

Anyone who is successful in this world does not want to invite competition. They may welcome competition but stop trying to think they will give you the keys to compete at their level. It must be earned. Listen to everything that you hear as advice and learn to read between the lines to work out the pieces of advice that are the truth. This advice is not cut and paste either; you need to learn how to make this your own and authentically apply this to your sales approach. This is how you will find your own style, and as a result you will find sustained success for as long as you want. You will also then (and only then) understand fully what I am saying here. Sales can be very enjoyable once you have figured out what works for you personally and what keeps you comfortable during a sales call; that is, when you remain yourself and not a trained circus monkey. Everyone today is smart and cautious toward salespeople, and most of your customers probably work in sales or have some level of sales training. Either way they know what they want, and they are weary before you have even entered the door. Face it, sales is not exactly a profession that has glowing reports of honesty.

In short: STOP being the robot! A quite common example of this is a statement pedaled to everyone starting out in the home service industry that asks "where the truck is parked" on every call. That phrase is so old and taught as a mandatory statement by sales training groups. Because of this, it is also widely known by customers, so when that statement is asked right away at the door your customer knows you're just another cookie-cutter salesperson. The only time I have ever used that statement about where my truck is parked is if it was genuinely warranted. If I were parking across a driveway, for example. Otherwise, lose the statement before you preemptively lose the sale. People have called me cynical many times in the past because I choose to challenge their instruction and suggestions rather than just simply follow. When approached the right way, this is not disrespectful–the intention is to really own what is being asked of you. Again, authenticity is critical here. If you blindly accept what is asked of you, it will never land, and you will never be able to fully commit. That's why I can present and sell an option and quite easily after the sale is made proceed to double or triple the amount. Most sales trainers teach that it's impossible and can't be done, or that it's too risky and that you should take the smaller sale. For an amateur that's yet to find their own voice and identity in this profession, these sales increases will be out of reach. Maybe you will strike it lucky every now and then, but it won't be sustainable, and your sales numbers will be telling. For someone who is not an amateur, has worked hard at developing their own style and is comfortable and in control, increasing the original sale two and three times in value after the original sale can be done very easily with no risk of losing the original sale.

Remember: Nothing at all is impossible in this world. Absolutely nothing. If it hasn't been done, find a way to do it!

If I listened to how many times I was told "no, that's wrong, you can't do that," I would still be scratching my head at a loss as to how I could get better. I am always listening and experimenting to find ways to improve and evolve. I personally have strong beliefs about being honest and respecting people. Both the narrow-minded and traditional sales trainers would say that prevents me from being successful in sales. I am proof otherwise. I have closed deals totaling millions, all while being honest and respectful and not listening when others said it was impossible. Never lose who you truly are in this or any job. Many will tell you that it is impossible to be totally honest and successful at the same time. Who are you listening to? What feels right for you? It's your choice!

You will experience something of a myth to most in the industry when you are honest and respectful. You will actually have customers who like and respect you back. Imagine that … a great feeling inside of pride and accomplishment. Your bank account and sales figures will thank you for taking this path too. I have had customers come up to me while travelling through airports with my family to say "hi" and introduce themselves to my family, as well as to thank me for taking care of their issues and to let me know how much better their life is in their home. Something they had believed for years was never possible after dealing with other salespeople. Reputation is everything and is a currency that customers trade in. You will actually now start to enjoy your job and your life and be very proud of what you do each day. No more feeling like a trained monkey. Instead, that respect you have for yourself and for your customers will fold into your success, increasing your momentum.

I have talked a lot about authentic behavior and the actions that create the success that follows this style of sales. When you hit this stride, you will also start adding value to the business you own or work for. Your marketing costs will begin to benefit significantly because now you have paying customers who actually like and respect you, and who will only give you their business going forward. AUTHENTICITY BREEDS LOYALTY. Repeat and referred customers who are willing to pay your rate no matter what it is are willing because of the trust and rapport they have built with you. I have lost count of how many times I have heard the statement from customers: "You are actually the most expensive, but that doesn't matter. You are the only person I trust to do my work. Nothing to do with the company or its advertising, you're the only reason I am willing to spend my money today." Don't underestimate the value this adds to your business. Repeat business is critical to bottom line delivery because the cost per lead is reduced. You're trading on reviews, which cost significantly less than generating new business with no connections. You also now have amazing 5-star reviews all over the internet. *All this from simply just being honest and true to yourself! Not a trained circus monkey!*

NOTES

NOTES

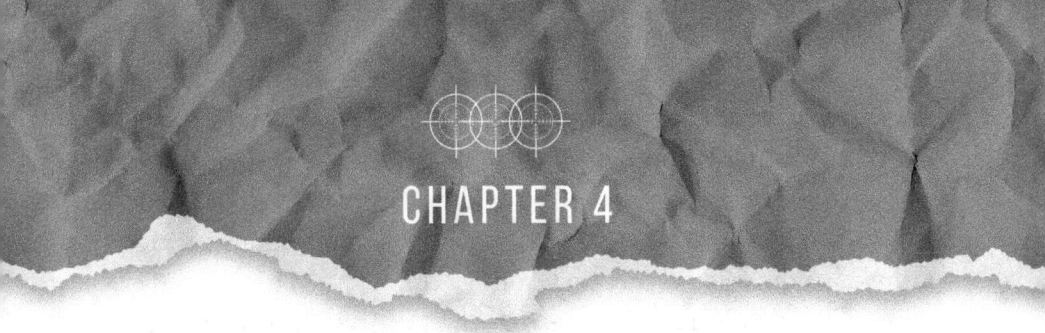

CHAPTER 4

STRATEGIC APPEARANCE

Strategic appearance can be crucial.

A lot of salespeople can make very basic mistakes in this area of subconscious sales.

It goes without saying that you want to make sure that you're wearing clothing appropriate to what you're selling, especially if you're in the cooling and heating industry. For example, in summertime you want to make sure you're wearing your short-sleeved shirt. Whether you wear shorts or trousers really doesn't make too much of a difference. Then, as the weather cools off, you're going to want to wear your trousers with a long-sleeved shirt. I would suggest you begin wearing your long-sleeved shirts even a bit before the cold weather truly arrives, as this will help subconsciously lead your customer to the thinking of needing to address cold weather heating requirements. By doing this basic task and paying this small amount of extra detail to your appearance, you will help put the customer in the desired frame of mind for what you're trying to sell. It may sound very simple, but usually the big differences are from the simple things that get overlooked. In fact, the small things often mark the difference between being an amateur and a true professional. At the end of the day this small detail could have an impact on whether or not you make that sale. For the heating and cooling industry, outdoor temperature variables can raise objections.

The customer's perception is everything and sets a tone that compliments all of the other steps that you should now be following. By simply preparing with strategic clothing options, you are subliminally queuing the customer to be thinking ahead to the season. A common example of this is when you go into a department store, and they are always using strategic temperature control by adjusting the air conditioning or the heat to subconsciously get you to purchase based on whatever they're selling. The sales associate is also dressed in the clothing options they are trying to sell. This strategy of strategic appearance and temperature control will many times drive you to buy your summer clothes when it's still in the later stages of winter outside. This is extremely effective. The department store is subconsciously having you think about purchasing more than one item by adjusting the temperature, which puts you in the frame of mind that they need you in to purchase summer clothes in the later stages of winter. Now, that's the same as trying to sell anything to a customer in their home, especially when it has to do with climate control. You obviously can't control the outdoor temperature to influence a customer's mind subconsciously to think about different seasons, but by understanding strategic clothing you can control and yield the same strategic results.

I learnt the need for such strategic, detailed evaluation and thinking through motorsport. When competing in a motor race you learn very quickly that you must account for every small detail if you plan on having any chance to win. Every single detail, no matter how small. If you have the opportunity to remove any of the possible variables in the garage or in pit lane, that is exactly what you do so your mind can be clear and focused during the race. These lessons are what helped me discover the importance of strategic appearance. When I began to evaluate my own sales calls, I realized I was not actively using strategic clothing and missing the opportunity to influence the customers' perception, and subconscious thoughts, to move it into the relevant space to what I was selling.

Remember: Remove all variables every chance you have to always maintain a clear mind!

CHAPTER 5

7 KEY ACTIONS TO COMPLETING A SALES CALL

Clearing up the myths as to why it's difficult to get to the next level of sales.

Now, you have been told over and over that there are one (or possibly two) correct ways to run a sales call. I have always called bullshit on this and challenged this way of thinking. I will share with you experiences and methods I have developed and tested, and which have proven to work for me and anyone I have trained in the field. I will start by saying one very important thing: Examine the way in which I have outlined to run a sales call and then modify it to suit you. If you don't run a sales call your specific way, you will never get to the next level.

ACTION 1:
BE COMPLETELY PREPARED.

Before you even enter the customer's neighborhood, make sure you have everything you need sorted and prepared to hit the ground running for a successful call. By this I mean make sure your vehicle is cleaned inside and out—no exceptions. You want your first impression to be professional before you even arrive at their home. Your vehicle is often a travelling business card and sets the tone for the type of organization you represent. Do not drive aggressively or speed through traffic on your way to the call, as the driver you cut off or speed past could potentially be your customer. You will have screwed yourself royally if you do cut off your customer. Another detail I recommend is if you wear sunglasses, never wear them to the customer's front door. This might not bother most customers but there are a small number who do not appreciate you (a stranger) wearing sunglasses at their front door. It can have a negative effect on these types of customers and to them it can show you as being cocky, arrogant, and disrespectful. Have your tablet, computer and/or paperwork organized in your vehicle so you can grab it swiftly as soon as you pull up or as needed. Do not waste time inside your vehicle once you arrive trying to find these items. Also, never pull up while on the phone and remain on the phone for an extended time parked in front of the customer's home. If you are on a phone call prior to arriving be sure to park out of sight of the customer's home to complete the call prior to pulling up to the customers' home.

Remember that most of your customers are watching you arrive and park even if you don't see them. They see you and form an opinion of you before you even knock on the front door.

They want to know that once you arrive at their home, they are the most important person from that moment until you leave. Even if one thing you do has the potential to offend one person before you even meet them at the front door, stop doing it immediately. You want to give yourself the best launching pad every time. With regards to parking your vehicle, I honestly don't prescribe any rules on where you park, with this exception:

never park on a driveway in case your vehicle develops an oil leak while parked and stains the customer's concrete.

As you can see, there are important steps to consider prior to even arriving at the customer's home. Being prepared allows you to feel confident and make the best first impression possible.

ACTION 2:
INITIAL INTERACTION.

Walk confidently to the customer's door. If there is a pathway to the front door, WALK ON IT! Do not walk on the customer's lawn if a pathway is available. Most people are proud of their lawn, and you are showing disrespect by walking on it. If no pathway is present, you can still generally walk down the driveway to the home. When you get to the front door, never ring the doorbell unless specifically directed to in the job notes. If the customer has young children who are sleeping the last thing you want to do is wake them up. When you knock, DO NOT knock on the door hard like a police officer would. Don't even knock on the front door at all. With most front doors it is possible to knock on the door jamb itself. You can safely knock firmly on the door jamb, which will produce a much more pleasant and welcoming sound rather than the loud, echoing holler from the front door. If you have knocked and have no answer, then either have your office call the customer's phone or call them yourself. Do not start knocking louder and louder. The customer could be home in the basement with bad hearing and be unable to hear the knock, or even be a little afraid to answer the door if they cannot see you clearly on a security camera, for example. A phone call is a much more appreciated and polite way to introduce yourself in these circumstances. Asking the office to call is preferred, as the customer is more likely to answer their call if the number is recognizable, and your cell phone is not. When this scenario occurs, the customer being home but not immediately answering the door is generally favorable to you. Now, immediately the customer will be showing empathy to you and apologizing.

At this point when you introduce yourself, remember this is very important. You must put your hand out and offer to shake the customer's hand while introducing yourself. If you don't like shaking a person's hand because you think you're going to get sick, get over it and get hand sanitizer. Don't disrespect the customer. Don't be stupid and squeeze a person's hand hard—just a simple, confident handshake is all that is needed. If the customer doesn't want to shake hands, that's not a problem, do not force them to shake hands. The offer from you is all that is needed. There is a small percentage of people though that won't shake hands. The reason this is very important is the second you shake a customer's hand and have contact you are immediately starting to change in the eyes of the customer from being a salesperson to a friend they can trust. All this from a simple handshake.

This is extremely important, as a simple handshake is one of the most accepted forms of greetings in all cultures and religions across the world.

So many forms of sales training will tell you to ask if your vehicle is parked okay as a way of showing empathy and respect. As I mentioned earlier, this is only needed in certain circumstances, or it is insincere. Handing the customer a business card right away at the front door is also trained as a required step. When I started out, I would religiously ask about my truck being parked okay and give a business card to the customer. I don't like the truck statement at all, as it makes you look like a robot and not a real person. Common sense and the discussion earlier in this book regarding how to make a strong first impression is enough for you to know where to park your truck. Of course, if the street has limited parking available, then again apply some common sense and check that you are not going to be an inconvenience being parked in the location you have chosen. The business card I am neither here nor there with. Some customers may look to get one from you as a form of identification, so have them on hand, but there is no pressing need to hand one over. In fact, it can come across as a very generic and robotic way of greeting a customer. If you notice something that stands out in the customer's front yard or near the front door, make a comment about it if you want. Whether you do or not will not make or break the call though. Mostly just greet the person as you would a friend. Just like you greet each friend differently you will greet each customer differently. If you simply focus on remembering to greet the customer properly then you are off to a good start. Another especially important part of the call is to have the customer start talking openly about themselves. This is where you can start to relate to the customer and build interaction. Don't even mention what you're there for just yet. If done properly you can put yourself in a good position to complete a sale before you even enter the home.

Most trainers will tell you to break the ice and start by stating a script similar to, "*The office has given me information regarding your requested ser-*

vice, etc." Now, if your goal is that you want to be a high performer, then start acting like one. Back yourself and be confident to talk to a stranger. This is what will set you apart from an amateur. The specifics of each initial greeting conversation need to come naturally and not feel rehearsed. Based on my experience, you generally should be talking for at least five minutes on general topics before you start to move into the specifics of the customer call. While talking, the customer will be put at ease by the conversation, and they will lose all the feelings of anxiety, stress, and doubts that they may be feeling. In sincerely doing this, you are starting to build trust with the customer. When you have achieved all this, that's when you can bring up the reason for your call and start to understand what the customer feels are their needs.

ACTION 3:
OBTAINING KEY INFORMATION.

Once you feel you have completed the second action and the customer is speaking comfortably, you can now begin to bring up the reason for being at the customer's home. Take control and move the call from the initial greeting phase to where you and your customer are having a light conversation. In a respectful but direct way ask the customer to, in their own words, explain the issues they are experiencing or think they are experiencing and the reason they rang and made an appointment. An important point here is to never rush the customer or talk over the customer, especially if they are using the wrong terminology to explain an issue you are familiar with. Once they have completed explaining the issues they are experiencing, ask them if there is anyone else in the household, i.e., a partner or roommate that has been experiencing the same, similar, or completely different issues with the system in the home.

This is a very important question, as when this is answered you can already have a complete understanding of who the decision maker(s) of the home are, which will be very important to understand when you are presenting pricing. Decision makers will often show themselves at this point in the call if they are present at home, even if they didn't answer the door in the first place. If the person who greeted you doesn't go and get them, or the other decision maker is unavailable or not home, the customer you are talking to will always mention the person in their response as having experienced the issue or not.

This will give you the confirmation you need in determining who the decision maker or makers are and if you may need to prepare yourself for the call to be rescheduled.

ACTION 4:
BUILD RAPPORT AND TRUST WHILE TAKING NOTES.

Be confident and ask the customer to walk you through their home and demonstrate the issues or show you what you're there to replace. For example, even if you are clearly there for an estimate, walking through the home with the customer will be a big help in not only getting a clear picture, but also establishing your credentials with the customer and why you will stand out when the time does come to proceed with the job. As you have the customer walk you through their home be sure to listen to the customer about what their concerns and requirements are, ask questions, and query any responses that may differ or need clarifying from their initial summary of the issue. This opens up much more time for the customer to build trust with you. If you notice things around their home that you are fully experienced to address, even if they're not part of why you're at the customer's home, don't be afraid to point these things out to the customer. Be sure to do this in a way that is professional and will not leave the customer feeling ashamed or embarrassed.

Also, while walking and talking to the customer, never forget to make constant notes!

By showing that you have the initiative to bring up the extra issues in a customer's home without being prompted confirms you're a real professional who has the experience to solve their issues confidently. I do not care if you have reservations about doing this. **DO IT!** There is no reason to be scared—that is amateur behavior. I have heard the weak excuse many times before from so-called experienced salespeople, worried that they will look like they are trying to increase their sales numbers by trying to fix things they were not asked to look at. This is absolute bullshit and a pathetic excuse.

You are the professional in your field, are you not? Or is the customer more experienced than you are at your own job?

I can tell you right now from experience: I do this and have always done this routinely. The customers are always happy when you show them something that can be a potential issue before it is an issue. The important difference is in the delivery. Be confident enough to increase your sales revenue when you can, beyond the initial call. You are in this to build a customer that will come back to you and refer you to others. This is not taking advantage; it is building a trusting relationship. Let's be honest here. You're not a charity worker who works for free. I have no issue reminding people of that fact from time to time. Each lead or call costs you a certain amount of money to obtain. So, if you're on any customer's call, no matter what it is, why wouldn't you want to increase that potential sales value where warranted?

This is a very basic opportunity to increase sales revenue but is basically overlooked by most because they are scared and have no confidence, thinking this may seem like an upsell pressure tactic. Yet they are always complaining as to why their numbers are low.

Remember: *If you don't seek out the opportunity you just won't get it.*

As you make notes of everything that you observe while walking through the customers' home, you can also decide when it comes time later how to put pricing packages together that incorporate these extra items. You can either bill the customer outright for each task or you may choose to do smaller items for no charge as an incentive to get the larger sale.

ACTION 5:
TIME ALLOCATION.

When looking over the initial reason you have been called to the home, be sure to spend more time discussing this than on any of the extra things you find walking through the home. *If you miss this critical time allocation, then everything you have done to this point has all been for nothing.* The reason this is so critical is because if you do not allocate more time up front to discuss the initial reason for the customer having you in their home, then you will not be seen as authentic and truthful in the customers' eyes. I agree with the customers' view here: you're just focused on your own personal gain and not providing the service that you promoted, a 'typical' salesperson who does not care about doing the right thing by their customer. You must allocate more time to this task because everything you have seen to this point should have been mentioned very briefly (that's why you must take notes), not discussed in detail. You never discuss anything in great detail until you have discussed the initial task. From the customer's point of view, you have not earned the right to discuss anything in detail until you have reviewed and addressed the initial task. The initial task is what is front and center for the customer, so give the customer the respect of showing what a professional you are and that you are capable of confidently solving all of their concerns and more. Show how your experience and professionalism can't be matched. Thoroughly inspect, diagnose, and make sure you don't leave any stone unturned when evaluating the initial reason for the call or the item you're estimating for replacement. Provide confirmation of why the issue occurred in the first place, or the reason an item needs replacing and items that need to be rectified to solve the issue. Once you see that you have earned the respect of the customer and you're both having easy conversation back and forth discussing potential next steps, this is the time to state:

"Just before I start to work out all of my final notes and put together different options based on everything we have discussed and agreed upon as being important, which of these various items I briefly mentioned to you earlier would you like to discuss and look at in more detail? So

that you can know the importance of taking care of these today (or, if an estimate) taken care of at time of install."

This is important, as it will have the customer open up and become further invested in you, giving you the ability to control the call and its outcome. Given you have already demonstrated your knowledge and expertise, they will ask directly for your guidance further at this point on the various extra items you noted. Now go through each item individually and discuss each of these in more detail. During these discussions with your customer, even though they asked you for guidance on what is most important and what further issues may occur if they don't fix these right away, they will still have some feelings about the urgency or "need" to complete these items. Generally, they won't openly discuss these feelings with you as they do not want to openly admit vulnerability when making a decision about any additional repairs or replacements. It is important that you take very close note of body language and the tone of answers given by the customer around each of these items while you're both discussing them. By paying attention to the customers' subconscious responses to your statements and questions you will learn which items are of actual importance to them.

Now, at this point it is also wise to start forming different options in your head about which items you should be including and billing for. Sometimes you will bill on top of the original issue for all extra items, but in other situations you might be forming options where you might be able to include an extra task at no cost to ensure you get the larger sale. This could be as simple as a toilet flapper at no cost. Such a small item only costing a few dollars will have absolutely no bearing on your bottom line when this is commonly a truck-stocked item and can be completed at the same time as the original task. In the customers' eyes, it will be greatly appreciated that you're so willing to make sure they are thoroughly taken care of.

As you are putting these options together in your head prior to actually formulating your options on paper or a tablet, you can also start to formulate which coupons/discounts (if any) you can put to the options that include the extra work tasks at no cost, like a toilet flapper. This will ensure your numbers still balance and you maintain your profit margin.

ACTION 6:
PREPARE OPTIONS WITH CUSTOMER.

Once you have finished thoroughly discussing all the additional items you earlier noted down, ask the customer to show you where the best place is for you to place down your note pad and/or tablet in their house so you can finalize the different options and pricing for them based on everything you both have discussed. Always invite them to sit or stay right by you as you put all the options and pricing together. This will differentiate you from everyone else, as you do not need to retreat to your truck or a place on your own at all.

Yes, that's right. What I am highlighting here is the complete opposite to what you have been trained to believe is the correct way to proceed at this point.

This is a very important action because it allows the customer to build more trust in you. They will sometimes be bewildered that you are not hiding your quotation process, like they have experienced, so your approach will stand out! This process says, "I have nothing to hide in this process and have been transparent from the time I came to the front door to start the call." I can say this statement because it's true. I do not ever go hide in a truck to build my options. By the time it comes to building my options I have already built them all in my head and have nothing to hide from the customer. Obviously, amateurs will keep hiding in their trucks. By building your options in front of the customer it will also give you extremely important face time to continue conversation to ease the anxiety the customer may start to build up inside themselves. This anxiety can even increase if you have discussed a number of extra items that they have not foreseen or budgeted for. Now, by talking as you're building options, you don't need to rush putting them together to present. Start building them and also at the same time ask questions loosely related in some way to your options to gauge different reactions as to which ones are received with a more positive response. This way you will start to get an understanding of any potential objections you may need to overcome if you want to have the customer purchase a package that is different to what they had initially indicated.

Flush out every objection possible at this stage, leading toward the package you are wanting to close the sale on so you can take advantage of the time you have created for yourself here. This makes it much more comfortable for you to overcome each objection without the customer even being aware that this is what is happening as you prepare for pricing discussions. No matter how big or small the objection is, it is always best to bring these out of the customer through natural conversation rather than be confronted with each objection unexpectedly. The customer will always appreciate this approach as it removes anxiety for them.

For me personally, and very importantly, the better-suited option does not always mean a higher dollar option. I always want to do what is the best option to solve all the present and future needs of each customer. All my options are built at my rates. Remember, you are building customer retention for longevity and success in this business.

During this process of asking questions, you should also be discussing highlights or important details you are including in your options that will directly benefit the customer. Especially items you feel that the customer will have a positive emotional reaction too. As a professional, you are basically selling the option you want to close the sale on by highlighting key benefits and features without yet referencing price. A further benefit of this approach is that it will help you further understand whether your customer is an emotional purchaser based on their reaction, or if they're analytical. Sometimes they can be a combination. This information about personality is key to determine as it will be the catalyst to how exactly you present and discuss your options later.

Through your guidance and approach the customer is subconsciously already purchasing without even realizing. Once you have completed this step successfully and you're confident you have removed possible objections and anxiety regarding your ideal option pricing and inclusions from the customer, you can now get ready to present your option proposal to the customer.

ACTION 7:
GUIDANCE AND AUTHORIZATION.

Proceed with presenting your options to your customer. A big difference you will pleasantly experience (as will your customer), is that the action of presenting options will be done with virtually no anxiety. The thorough leg work you completed earlier in preparing the customer for the preferred option and recommendation of inclusions and package pricing offers will pay back dividends in giving you a more receptive environment to present in. This should also bolster your confidence, as when you as the salesperson are feeling anxious, you will subconsciously project this anxiety onto the customer through your words and body language. If you have completed the sixth step in my process correctly, the presentation of options should flow seamlessly through casual conversation with your customer.

As you now navigate the customer through your options, you are not being viewed as a typical salesperson, there to try and take as much money as possible from the customer without care. Rather, you are seen as being a true professional and a friend, truthfully there to help solve their issues. Once you can master being viewed this way, price as an objection is removed completely and the customer will speak openly with you about the different inclusions in each option, seeking your guidance as to which option you believe is the most appropriate. This has all occurred because you have taken the time and laid the foundation. Because you have completed all previous steps as a professional and not an amateur, the customer will choose the option you have recommended.

Yes, that's exactly right. I will repeat. The customer will choose the option you have recommended!

A true professional who operates with a customer's needs and requirements in mind will achieve this success every time. Presenting your options will now become an enjoyable part of your sales call due to the fact that your personal anxiety doesn't exist at the time of presenting options anymore. A point I want to make here is with regards to the sales training programs out there that are wanting everyone to act like trained circus monkeys. They may be saying that there is only one way to present options (from highest price to lowest price) and I am sure they can give you some offhanded reason why this makes sense and is the best way to present to a customer. I can, from all my experience, tell you it makes absolutely **NO DIFFERENCE which way you present**. When you behave like a true professional and complete every part of a call as I have outlined, it makes absolutely no difference how you choose to present your pricing.

The reason it makes no difference is because you now are a professional and have built confidence with the customer. There is no underhanded ulterior motive and the customer is not actively looking for "your trick." You are now viewed as a trusted friend and will have a recurring customer. As we all know, the cost of making the phone ring can be high and competitive in the current marketplace. Investing the time and effort that has been outlined allows you to pave the way for sustained customer retention, customer recommendation, and repeat sales. You will continue to increase your sales revenue in the most sustainable way possible. Not only will you have a customer for life, but they will actively recommend your services to all friends and family. There is nothing customers like better than to share their success of a great experience. Your single sales lead just multiplied your revenue and income without increasing your organization's cost-per-sale ratio. I can honestly say I have had great success with this approach and will even today have customers from five years ago call in for repeat work–no other quotations, just a green light to proceed with the work. The word-of-mouth referrals will outpace the need to be handing out business cards every time you meet a customer. The amount a person has paid you for your service, no matter even if higher than they initially expected, is completely irrelevant to them because of the first-class experience that was given.

Remember: Follow these simple actions when running your sales call and you will begin to experience the same high sales revenues with customers who are happy to pay your bill and proactively refer you to their friends and families. True, sustainable sales and success.

CHAPTER 6

ADAPTABILITY

Adaptability is vital.

Something that I have learned during my time in sales is that you must remain adaptable. I stress **adaptable**, in every sense of the word regardless of the stage of the call that you find yourself in. Whilst this book outlines steps for you to take to be successful, you must understand that these are not a prescription to be completed, they are a framework in which you apply your own personality, experience, market conditions, etc. in order to adapt these to be optimized in the environment you find yourself in.

I've seen many times before where people are rigid and unwavering to a certain process they have been shown or told to follow in order to be successful. You have these amateurs out there that want to follow it to the extreme detail, where they are too scared to deviate from what they have been told to do. Now don't get me wrong, for some salespeople this is where they are comfortable and can earn an amount of revenue that gets their bills paid. If that's sufficient for you, then this book is not going to be beneficial unless you are willing to strive for more and really want to stop being mediocre and frustrated each day. Do some thinking for yourself and be an individual. You must be truly adaptable in this world to be successful. Life changes very quickly and you need to be agile. A simple Google search of the most popular management styles will talk about agile and adaptable workplaces–sales is not immune to this approach to multi-tasking, removing waste from business processes, and being able to change to the market need. Adaptability in your approach is how you will be a sales **professional** with much higher sales revenue than you've ever thought possible.

This is the truth no one is telling you. I can even show you things and tell you things that work for me but for you to truly reach your peak you must take my advice and suggestions and make them your own.

When you're walking through a home with a customer and you're confident that you've done all your notes methodically and you've ticked every box, always be prepared for that curveball, left-of-field question, or statement. Sometimes this question or statement might just take the entire call in a different direction. Even if you're at the point where you think you've got the sale verbally ready to close, you've presented your options, you've done all the great work expected and have gotten the approval and sold the call, unfortunately, on occasion, a lot of these calls in sales are dependent on finance approval for payment. So, I ask you, what are you going to do when the finance doesn't get approved?

What are you going to do when they don't get the correct amount of money approved?

You see the look in the customer's face: they're embarrassed. A lot of times it can be quite awkward when finance doesn't get approved, whether partially or completely. When this happens, the customer often has the initial instinct to close everything down, end the call and have you leave so the embarrassment leaves with you out of their home. It's really not your fault that they didn't get approved, and the customer knows that, but they're looking at you because you're the one that ran the credit application for them. You're the one that told them they could have all of this, and you emotionally sold them on everything. I've seen it too many times where you'll see a salesperson who thinks they're great at sales get into this situation and they have absolutely no idea what to do. It simply ends up being very uncomfortable for everyone. It is important to stay level-headed and in control, and if the customer truly wants that option, do not be afraid to ask them if they have another means to pay for the option. If they really want the option, they will openly suggest how they can potentially finance or pay for the transaction an alternate way. You may also have suggestions for alternative options that may be available. I have had a situation like this where a person earning above $300,000 per year was denied finance for a very menial amount (comparatively). The customer was angry about the finance denial. I admit I was surprised, but I definitely did not let the call end even though the customer was angry with the finance company. I talked through other options of how the customer might be able to pay for the work, we found a solution that worked for him, and his family and I closed the sale and completed the work. As long as you've done your job correctly during the entire call, customers will have such a strong emotional connection to the option they proposed to purchase that you'll be surprised how resourceful people can be when they actually really want something. People make purchases every day of the week which can stretch their budget. At the end of the day, you're not a finance broker, you're simply there to solve the customers' needs and present solutions to them, exactly what they asked for and want. You do not know their finances, so definitely have empathy for a customer in this situation; however, you should always present everything you feel relevant to present regardless of cost.

Now, let's say they only get approval for part of the work. What are you going to do? Are you going to walk out of there with your tail between your legs, all disgruntled and angry, with zero revenue? Or are you going to actually work through it with the customer to find a solution? You need to remember to rationalize that all you're dealing with is another problem or objection to remove. Every problem ultimately has a solution. Your controlled emotional approach will reduce the heightened emotions that the customer may be feeling and allows everyone involved to further explore potential solutions without anxiety. It's important to keep the customer level-headed and moving forward with the sale. An alternate course of action if you find yourself in a position where the customer can't get approved for the amount of money they need is that you may need the customer to look closer at their proposed solution package and decide what are the "must haves" and the "nice to haves."

A simple solution is if you're able to take certain things out depending on the amount of money they got approved for. The difference may not be too much, and it could just be a quick resolve for all involved. It might be an item so low in cost that you can throw it in at no cost to close the larger sale. If suitable, perhaps you simply suggest they move to the option that suits their budget. There is almost always an option that suits everyone's budget. Most customers will go for this suggestion because at this point, they are vulnerable and embarrassed.

Prior to having a customer fill in an application for finance, just ask them straight up what their credit is like. If they tell you they've got good credit and that they expect to be approved, then that customer is going to proceed with an alternate suggested option based on the limit they got approved for. This is because they have already committed psychologically and emotionally to the purchase, and to you they made an outwardly verbal commitment that their credit would be approved. So now you just simply work through and find an option that fits within their budget. *You just adapt.*

Another situation where adaptability is important is when you might have sold and closed the sale, but you turn up to do the work and, for whatever reason, it actually can't go as planned. No matter how thorough you are, there are times where unforeseen challenges come about. When this happens, don't try to hide this fact from the customer; this is a very key point once you've worked out that you're going to have to adapt and change the scope of the work.

You need to remember when you were at the call originally, where both you and the customer spoke in detail about various options and features, so you know exactly what the customer wanted originally. You also need to know the budget and what fits in with the budget, so make sure you formulate options in your head ready to go before you even talk to the customer.

Quite often you can keep the sale at the same price and substitute certain items in and out very easily. So don't be anxious or worried to tell the customer straight up that there has been an issue identified that could potentially alter the work scope. The relationship that you have built with this customer—the honesty and transparency along with the experience that you have already demonstrated—will allow the customer to feel confidence in your recommendations for how best to adapt and deliver the best possible outcome. Explain that you had no idea this is what was going to be discovered and give straightforward, tangible reasons why. The customer will be more willing to continue with any changes, as they have already committed to the finance, so to them it's not a big issue to continue to progress with reasonable changes.

On the flip side, I can tell you of a firsthand example where I had a job sold for a certain amount of money, and then when I had a co-worker check in on the job, he informed me that what I had packaged for the customer could not go ahead exactly the way that I had sold it. There's no need to freak out, so I calmly turned around and spoke to the customer about the situation. In doing so, I altered the scope and tripled the sale of that ticket because I already knew the customer well enough to know how to restructure the original call scope to now open the possibility of selling much more than was originally agreed to.

Remember: *Always remain positive, in control and adaptable.*

I was able to turn this potentially negative scenario into a positive outcome because I mentally built options prior to talking to the customer and reapportioned some of the money that was supposed to be spent on a certain task. Then, it was increased even more by a simple suggestion which solved another major issue that the customer was talking about at the initial time of the original estimate.

Now that the scope had changed when I made the suggestion to adapt, increase work, and alter, he was one hundred percent on board to solve his other issue. It is also worth noting that this call started as a free estimate!

Adaptability is key in salvaging a situation which might end up in loss of the sale. You need to be prepared, know your customer, and know your options.

Another situation to ponder is the scenario when secondary decision makers enter the call, and you find yourself halfway through the call presenting options when this person comes home not knowing the details of what you're presenting and discussing. They could have completely different issues, concerns, goals, and thoughts on outcomes to the person you're currently speaking with. Even right in the middle of your presentation, you can find yourself having to alter and adapt your options to address the new issues and concerns you have now been made aware of. You'll need to use the skills that I mentioned earlier of incorporating these new and additional considerations into your proposal, all whilst continuing to direct your presentation at both people. It is very important that you're able to seamlessly adapt without hesitation to this situation and maintain control of the call and your emotions. You might have to write the options a number of times, but ultimately, don't be scared or concerned about this scenario and facing the curve ball head on. The value of adjusting your options and getting this right will get you the highest dollar value on your ticket.

Now, you may also get the customer pre-approved for finance and the approval amount is double or even triple the value of the amount applied for. At that point, if you did your job correctly as you walked around, and you had been talking to the customer, you would know other things that they actually would like, so don't be scared to suggest they may want to revisit the possibility of including these extra items. Make a statement similar to: "You know what, I am actually just going to change some things around with your option here and let's just see how this all works out so you can potentially have the items you thought you would have to wait for given your extra approval amount, okay?"

Put some new options together and incentivize the customer. Remember, you are just presenting–you are not forcing anyone to do anything, so make sure you present everything you can and allow them to feel comfortable making that final decision.

For me, learning how to be adaptable came before I even started doing sales. All of that came from when I decided to start motor racing. When racing, you could be in a race and out front leading, then all of a sudden you could be at the back of the pack, potentially through no fault of your own. If you're not adaptable in motor racing, you had better become comfortable with being last because that's where you will remain. You need to work on how to get back to the front, understanding the factors at play, so your entire game plan needs to be flexible. You've gone from maintaining and sustaining, to staying on course for the win, to attacking at every opportunity so you can get back to the front and taking calculated risks along the way to winning. These are important lessons which have helped me tremendously in sales.

In motor racing, you learn there are factors that are both in and out of your control. You may have a team in the background for support, but ultimately, you're the driver, you're in control and you have the wheel in your hands. You need to in a split second adapt and make decisions. These are skills that have to be learned, so don't think this is easy and don't think you're going to get it right on the first sales call you're on. In actual fact, the more times you learn through trial and error the better at adaptability you will become. Don't be disillusioned from making mistakes, learn from them. When moments like finance denial happen during a call, it can make most anxious and frustrated, resulting in a lot of people just walking away from the sales call altogether and never putting in the extra effort to still close the sale. They have allowed their emotions to control them, rather than controlling their emotions, and have failed. I can tell you right now that those salespeople who control their emotions are making the big sales revenues that you strive to match (and beat) are all capable of staying in control and level-headed. Adapt to the situation, change the options completely when warranted, and still walk away with the revenue because at the end of the day, that's what it's all about and that is what you have worked hard for.

It's about making the customer happy, earning the sale, getting the revenue, and enjoying your job. Walking away without the sale and without the revenue is no way to enjoy your job. It's no way to help the customer. It's just a frustrating existence, so it's about time you learned how to be professional and get what you're capable of achieving.

Remember: Go and get it and always remember not to be scared to be adaptable.

NOTES

NOTES

CHAPTER 7

A MEMORABLE SALES EXPERIENCE

These are two words (sales experience) that most don't realize are intrinsically linked. I will cover in this section how important the right experience is to your customers, which can have a profound impact on your sales success. This is one of the most important areas where you can show how unique you are when compared to your competition.

This very point is often missed by many: you're not just there to propose a product at a price. You are also creating an experience for your customers. Everything you do and your manner when in front of a customer is an experience. When you ask a customer if they would be willing to write you a review, they will describe their experience. So, I ask, if you are building your business or personal reputation and this is driven by reviews, which are social media currency for most businesses these days, then why are you not considering and managing your sales calls as an experience? Why is it that everyone is acting like an amateur and not giving the experience of the sales process any attention? I see it commonly missed in sales training and professional development courses. You are ignoring the experience at your own loss, as referrals are one of the greatest revenue sources for any business. They are essentially a low-cost lead and can generate a positive brand appeal for new customers.

When you go to a concert or a play or show of any kind, you're going to the event anticipating a certain experience, and if that experience meets or exceeds your expectations you will certainly talk about this positive feeling with your friends and family. Not to mention, you will have no hesitation attending again or recommending others to attend. I realized the importance of providing an experience prior to working in sales, during motor racing. I was simply there because I have a passion for motor racing, but you learn as a driver that you are part of something bigger–you are part of the overall entertainment value in every race event. The power of the experience can also be applied in sales, where your ability to create an experience that meets and exceeds the customers' expectations will set you apart. When you accept this and grow your ability to be able to create an unparalleled experience, you will be pleasantly surprised with the ease with which the entire sales process starts to flow. Granted there are components of your customers' experience that are outside of your control. The initial booking will be with another person from your organization, who makes a first impression. And if we're being honest, this can sometimes work against you if it wasn't done professionally. However, you do have control of your first impression and the experience from that point forward, so you must make sure everything, from the moment you are in contact with your customer, is first class and a true top-notch experience. I reinforce the importance of being completely present and professional, as you want to remove any anxiety that the customer may be feeling, along with any hesitation.

When following my process as you run your call, you are provided with many opportunities to achieve a distinct and professional experience for your customer. You are no longer burning through the call; you are in control and the customer is delighted and ready to spend money with you. Feelings of anxiety and hesitation are very typical feelings most people have when needing to make a purchase, especially if you work in an industry where people are making a purchase out of necessity, rather than out of a feeling of want. A common example of a similar situation is visiting the dentist. Personally, I have no issue with going to the dentist, but every so often you will hear of people who hate going to the dentist. Now, no disrespect to dentists, but there is a stigma and reputation of the experience that really drives why people feel this way. Truly, the only difference between those who hate going to the dentist and those who have no issue is their experience. At some point someone had a bad experience which led to anxiety, and no dentist since has been able to overcome that bad experience.

When a customer is purchasing because they want to purchase, this is already something positive in their mind, and psychologically, they are giving you a great platform to start the experience from. Now conversely, when a customer is buying out of necessity, regardless of if they have the financial resources or not, they are likely to be in a negative place, since no one wants to spend money if they can avoid it. This is where a lot of amateurs and even a lot of successful salespeople falter with the experience. They never address or tailor the experience for the customer to eradicate this negative feeling. If you don't acknowledge the negative sentiment and work to overcome this, you might be lucky to achieve the initial approval for the work to proceed, but that doesn't mean the customer is truly wanting to proceed. Ultimately, a lot of these jobs are cancelled. The way most will choose to try and overcome this failure is to employ a strategy of starting work immediately, today, thinking this will lock the customer in and avoid any form of cancellation. Anyone that employs this cheap strategy is behaving insecurely with no authenticity, and really cementing the reason your customer has such negative feelings toward you and the experience of sales—and their feelings are right. You need to work hard and develop yourself to be the standout exception right from the initial contact with the customer. You are responsible for removing the negativity from this experience and previous experiences, just like the dentist.

The robotic sales training that you are receiving to say certain things to overcome these negative objections at certain points during sales calls are failing you, and it's about time you realized the only reason you're getting these objections in the first place is because the customer is having a bad experience. Once you start facilitating a more positive experience for your customer, removing all negativity in a positive manner, you can walk away with the customer's approval, knowing they will not cancel, no matter how far out the work is scheduled. I am speaking from experience when I say my customers do not routinely cancel jobs and I schedule work weeks and months out from the initial sale date with complete confidence. They don't cancel because I make sure every sales call is a positive experience. I have genuinely lost count of the number of times I have been told by customers that they choose to work with me due to my knowledge, thoroughness, and the overall positive experience they receive. Plus, they also don't feel pressured or rushed. They choose to pay my price because it becomes more than just the task—it is also about the positive experience.

I learned very early on in my sales career to put a big focus on the overall experience of every call I run. I realized that the robotic approach that many sales training programs teach was not going to be successful in the long term for me, and certainly didn't feel authentic.

No two people are the same and no two homes or sales situations are the same, so stop taking a cookie-cutter approach to providing an experience to your sales. Doing this will never address the unspoken issue of the anxiety from previous negative experiences that is leading to the customers' objections, overall hesitation, and negative feelings during the call. Stop being lazy and open your eyes. Accept that this is not easy and requires hard work and may make you feel uncomfortable at times. Unless you start becoming skilled in reading the room quickly and understanding the nuances of different personalities, you will fail at creating the experience necessary to be successful.

Something to try on occasion that works is well placed humor. Everyone loves to laugh and smile when it's natural and not forced upon them.

Experience doesn't just sit within the initial call/sale. Do not make the mistake of thinking you have completed all that you need to at this point. You may have successfully secured your sale and are ready to get that work underway; however, the experience you are providing the customer does not end until everything is complete and finished. You must be involved in all stages of the work being completed and finalized, even if you are physically not responsible for installation or repair. This involvement does not need to necessarily mean you have to be present at the job—it may be simply enough to make a phone call to check in. You need to make sure the customer is completely comfortable with whom is in their home and that they have your assurance that the experience will continue to be positive and that the trust you have built will be maintained.

The customer will subconsciously, even if they don't say this to you verbally, always have some anxiety toward the people in their home until a trusted person like yourself assures them that you take full responsibility for them and have complete trust in them. This requires you to also spend time building your team, ensuring that they share the same philosophy of customer experience and professionalism, and that you have set them up for success. They should understand the need for managing customer expectations and how to manage any curve balls that can often derail product installation or works being carried out.

This extra involvement and attention to all aspects of the call, including installation, is how you provide an exceptional experience for the customer, and it is what is going to make you stand out against all the others out there trying to compete with you. This is how you leave the customer with an exceptionally high level of trust and respect for you, and this is how you keep getting repeat business and referrals. This is how you build your revenue, and this is how you make your business sustainably successful

Remember: Never, <u>ever</u> underestimate how important the overall experience you provide to every customer is worth, to both them and you.

CHAPTER 8

THE GOLDEN RULE TO BE BROKEN

Making conversation with your customers is key to building trust and rapport; however, you are always given a golden rule that must be followed by all. Even first-timers to sales can confidently tell you the golden rule:

Never talk about two things with a customer, no matter what the situation: *religion* or *politics.*

I am here to tell you to feel free to stand by and follow the golden rule as an amateur while you continue to lose sales to certain customers. The experienced salespeople who you ask for advice and training who tell you to follow the golden rule are not giving you the whole truth. They will break it every time it's warranted. I do the same thing.

I do not follow this golden rule.

I won't lie to you; I did follow this rule when I was starting out, but then I began to question it, as I always question everything. After really thinking about the rule and what it meant to me personally, I decided to screw the rule! If I think it's important or natural to discuss either politics or religion with a customer to make them feel comfortable with me being open and honest, then I will. I am not telling you to be combative; again, if you are not sure then I would not recommend doing this. Religion and politics are extremely important to many people in this world. The key is to remain respectful and speak honestly. I have broken this golden rule constantly and closed many sales along the way. Many of which have resulted in repeat clients happily paying my rate.

This is just another example of being authentic and brave. Stop being scared to be yourself during a sales call. It's up to you to grab control and not let go. It's up to you to make the sale, or let's face it, you will be living in a world of regret with no answers to your questions. You have hopefully picked up by this stage that keeping things simple is a repetitive theme in this book. Don't regret your actions when it is too late. Hindsight is not a great thing–it is a brutal thing. How can you seriously not talk about politics when you see a framed letter signed by a president on a person's wall? Or if the country is in the middle of a presidential election and your customer has advertising on their lawn? I use these as examples, as it's something I am sure you have already come across. *Am I the only curious person in the world that would love to know more?* This almost always becomes the elephant in the room.

Most of you would be too scared to ask questions because of the so-called golden rule. Questions are what make you personable and are what progresses the sale. Questions are where you gain respect because it gives you the chance to discuss something that the customer is passionate about. You will get to understand the customer at a more personal level, also discovering there are amazing and interesting people in the world that you are extremely lucky to meet all through just doing your job.

I cannot say it enough–stop being scared and go for it!

I want, however, to add one small note of caution. Before you do go and start talking about religion and politics, remember that you yourself must always be respectful and open-minded. If you still want to make the sale, you need to remember that on occasions your customers' views may clash with your own. You must be polite and respectful to their views as well as honor your own. Allow them to speak their mind freely and get their point across no matter how confronting–remember, you are in their home. That is very important as this will allow them to be completely relaxed and invested in your conversation, and soon the sale will result as a natural progression so they can keep the conversation going with you. By no means am I saying you must agree with them at all. You can't hold an engaging conversation if all you do is say, "Yes I agree." The insincerity will be evident. Just be respectful in your responses if you want to make the sale today is all I am saying. Everyone just wants respect and to be heard, which is a very simple thing for an honest person to give.

This attitude of "take charge and screw the golden rule" with this type of customer, especially on a free estimate call where the customer is getting multiple estimates, gives you a huge advantage to winning the job. It's highly likely that the golden rule will be followed by those that follow you on the sales call, as only a very small percentage are confident and don't follow the rule. This will result in you being the only person the customer relates to and trusts, even if you had conflicting views with the customer on religion and/or politics. You still, as a result, gain trust and respect by being yourself. Be brave enough to talk religion and politics.

I will throw up a couple scenarios to think about so you can question yourself on how relevant you believe the golden rule to be in the world today.

If you start a general conversation outside of a sales call with a person and you discover they are a pastor or a priest, are you going to ask a religious question? Or will you share your own personal beliefs or experiences?

I ask the same type of question when it comes to meeting a congressman or governor. Are you going to ask a political question? Would you share your views or experiences in a respectful but engaging way?

If you answered yes to the above examples, then you need to ask yourself what's holding you back on a sales call. You need to acknowledge these barriers that are making you uncomfortable. Is it that you're nervous about the outcome or concerned you don't know enough about the topic? Understand these barriers and work at getting comfortable with being uncomfortable. Stop being a trained circus monkey. Get comfortable and be yourself!

Remember: Talk religion and politics with any customer where it is warranted and makes sense. Be smart, confident and stop being scared!

CHAPTER 9

THE CUSTOMER IS NOT ALWAYS RIGHT

This is a progressive concept you need to build up to, in order to fully accept and be ready to challenge this statement–it's controversial for many who are scared to question the status quo.

When you are setting out in sales, yes, the statement of the customer always being right is something you generally follow without question. It doesn't appear to cause you any issues, and in many cases possibly makes your life in sales easy. After all, isn't that really what sales is all about? Just sell, sell, sell at any cost. And no matter what, just agree with the customer and get the sale.

Let me just challenge your thinking on this. Sales is not simply about selling at any cost, and in many circumstances, the customer doesn't have a clue what they actually need to solve their issue or need.

Let me ask you how many times you have had a sale that you thought went great. You gave the customer exactly what they were asking for and you didn't even try to steer them in any other possible direction during the sale. Even though some of the things they were asking for were not suited to their situation, you chose to simply sell, go along, and agree in order to make the sale, as that's what you were there to do. Going through a transaction like this example because you simply went with the notion that the customer is always right is actually a huge mistake and disservice to your customer. It's also pure laziness. Instead, you potentially could have tried to do the right thing and educate the customer on the right product or service and come up against an objection. If that happened and you gave up, then you failed. True professionals do not give up. A "customer-is-always-right sale" like the above example surprisingly ends in a disaster within a very short period of the sale being completed. When you stop being an amateur (whether that is through time or personal growth) you will start to understand and share this view. I have been told in the past that "imposing" my view on the customer is incorrect and completely wrong. I have been told never to do this, just as you have been told the same by your peers.

Yes, it's easier to be complicit and to go with the flow–but the truth is, you will miss your opportunity to be authentic and to really connect with your customer. The difference is I decided I will not be an amateur anymore and begin to question this easy way out when dealing with customers. As an amateur, you are more than likely following the tried and proven method of sales, but are they really proven? The answer is yes if you only aim to achieve mediocre sales and not truly excel in your profession. The answer is no if you are really serious about being successful in this field and standing out amongst a crowd of robots all doing the same thing. No matter if I made the sale or not, when I was starting out, I would follow processes just like everyone else time and time again, sale after sale. I would sit in the middle of the pack (at best) and wonder why I wasn't breaking through. *Well, now it's time to change things up and think for yourself. It's your time to have that same breakthrough.*

The minute I made that conscious decision and stopped following the easy way out of just blindly accepting the customer was always right and became ballsy and confident enough to challenge customers on what they were asking for and why, something amazing happened. The key is to acknowledge that the words that are used in cookie-cutter training sessions immediately give you this negative connotation and you shy away. "Challenge" and "impose" immediately make you think that you are aggressively forcing something onto the customer. Aka: that you are being rude and confrontational. In actual fact, challenge is healthy, and if you ever look at leadership case studies, they openly encourage healthy and productive challenge, which is the key to what I am saying to you here. I am actually making my customers more than happy because I am not imposing my views but rather, I am having a thorough discussion with my customer, getting to the root cause of their needs and cutting through any of the misconceptions that they may have about the situation, the solution, your business and you! Remember that you are the person with the industry knowledge, training, and experience. The customer is expecting you to help guide them to the best product or service to suit their needs, even if at first it doesn't seem that way. If all you do is simply give them the service or product they ask for without a thorough discussion, how do you even know if the product is the right fit? You are in a sense hoping the customer did your job correctly and researched everything for you. You're just being lazy when you believe the customer is always right. What then makes you different from the twenty other salespeople who came to the door?

Another issue that comes from believing the customer is always right is the issue of call backs, refunds, and terrible online reviews. You might think everything is sunshine and roses because you made a sale. You left the customer happy with what they selected and you closed in record time, right? But this can easily turn to doom and gloom because you didn't offer the customer something that was best suited to them or their situation. You were not ballsy or confident, you phoned it in and that shows to everyone, especially the customer. What you sold them didn't work and now they want to know why. They're looking at you as a lazy amateur who took their money and didn't deliver despite all your promises. Funny how that works. Now they are blaming you for their bad decision. What are you going to do now? Tell them the truth, that you knew it wouldn't work but were too scared to challenge them and just wanted to make a sale at any cost? A real disaster situation. That's how it plays out every time without exception. Why not stop it from becoming a train wreck in the first place and really question the customer, since they are not always right.

Being a professional and understanding the difference is doing your job properly and is really not that complicated. Be honest and spend your time and energy in questioning the customer to find the right solution, no matter how resolute the customer may be in getting a certain outcome that they think is right. I don't care about the situation or circumstances—you must stay true to and confident in the industry knowledge and experience you have. If you are starting out, then work hard at getting experience. Build relationships with experts in the field that you can lean into when you need. You are the professional—that's why the customer is talking to you!

An example: If you are talking with a customer and they believe they are one hundred percent correct for whatever reason and that the product they have chosen is perfect for them and will work for all their needs . . . but you know this isn't the case and they are saying you are wrong and not willing to look at industry testing results and expertise. They are completely closed off to discussing anything other than their opinion.

BUT remember, I have not mentioned anything about money because what I am about to suggest is not a decision based on money. If the product this customer is wanting will do everything they need and want but you're simply showing them a product of higher value which will solve the exact same needs and wants, then you are genuinely not in a position to force the more expensive product on the customer without expecting resistance from the customer. This comes back to trust and meeting the customer's needs in the best way. Just make sure the product they have chosen will at minimum solve the customer's needs and give them the outcome they are looking for.

However, per the example above when you cave to a customer de-manding an unsuitable product, you will provide a product or service that will not work, and you will have opened yourself up to poor reviews and a dissatisfied customer when the product and service fails to meet expecta-tions. I suggest you simply be confident and honest. If they are not open to exploring industry-proven solutions that you can provide for an optimized outcome for them, respectfully decline to discuss the work any further and suggest the customer find someone else who is willing to provide the service or sale. Explain you are not in business to just sell at any cost (crazy right?!) and that your main concern is to make sure your customers' needs are met and **exceeded** every time, without exception. And that this is why your customers write great online reviews and call you for repeat work over and over and refer you to family and friends.

Then simply pause and wait ...

Within a few seconds you will see your customers' true colors and get a glimpse into the future of how they will react when asking for a refund. The emotion of frustration they did have with you at this point is now disappearing, and their confidence of talking down and direct to you and controlling the conversation has just disappeared. They are now open and wanting to listen and have you help them and complete the transaction of providing a suitable product or service. Simply by being honest and confident to walk away is a demonstration that no matter what the customer thought, they actually never had control of the situation–you were simply being polite and allowing them to think they did while you listened to them. It is clear now that you're in control. Now you can continue to build options you want to build and discuss in the way you want to discuss, and you will now have another very happy customer as you complete the transaction.

I have the lowest (non-existent) call back rate compared to industry peers because this is my approach EVERY SINGLE TIME.

On the flip side, you must remember that not everyone is the same. If, after making the declaration that you are willing to walk away and the customer, after a few seconds, did not give any indication that they wanted to discuss further, you need to simply ask one more time as a confirmation if they are willing to discuss further your concerns about why they need a different product or service. Pause again and wait for a reply. They could say, "No, I am not."

At which point you say, "I thank you for your time but will allow another person or company to give you what you want." Leave it at that, direct, straight to the point.

The key is that by doing this you have remained professional and not burnt any bridges. Do not be angry at yourself–you need to remember that you don't want every customer in this world as your customer. Never compromise on your beliefs. You must stay consistent and true to yourself on every call. That is how you stay in control and can successfully build on the majority of people who are your target customer. This can be difficult when you are under pressure to meet sales targets, but burning time trying to convince a customer or doing triage on a call that you should have walked away from rather than caving in, will cause you to lose time that could be spent converting actual sales. Both will actually make you less successful and cost your business more money. Have the confidence to make the call that this is not a win-win for either of you.

Alternatively, if after making your second statement to confirm they're free to use a different company, and when you paused and waited for a response, they instead gave a response like, "I think I..." At that point, stop them from completing the sentence and be upfront in suggesting you leave them with literature they can read over, as you understand completely that making a decision of this size can be overwhelming. Ultimately, they were expecting one thing and researched it very well, but now you have changed what they were expecting, which for anyone can be a little confusing. Set a new time for everyone to return to start the call again. Reset the call for a time period within 48 hours. This will give little time to have another company come in and be successful with their bid. You have just made them question their thoughts and, if analytical, they will need a minimum of 24 hours on their own to process all the information they have been given. Then, when you return, they will be ready to listen and engage with questions. Also suggest that in the first 24-hour period you will gather more information to send them via email to read through prior to your return. This little strategy of sending extra information keeps you relevant in their minds, as if the call never really got rescheduled. Keeping the information light and not deep in technical detail in your follow up email is all that is needed. You ultimately just became one long call over multiple days. It is important that you were the one resetting this call, which is why I said to not let them finish the sentence to reschedule. It needs to be seen as your idea, which will already set you up to be in control when you return.

As you can see, there are various factors at play when you need to challenge a customer but remember: You MUST always remain respectful to all customers no matter their opinion.

Remember: THE CUSTOMER IS NOT ALWAYS RIGHT! IT'S YOUR BUSINESS, NOT THEIRS. RUN IT YOUR WAY AND ONLY YOUR WAY!

NOTES

NOTES

NOTES

CHAPTER 10

IMPROVE YOUR CLOSE RATE

The most consistent question I receive from other salespeople is how to increase their close rate and remain consistently successful week after week. Over the years, I have developed my own way of achieving this level of success. It has not come overnight and is a constant process of adaptation and understanding changes to the market, product offerings and customer needs.

Knowledge is key, alongside a willingness to be authentic and honest. Not looking for quick success is also an important factor. Stop thinking every call you go on is a quick way to simply fleece as much money as you can. That should not be your objective, and it certainly should not be your organization's either. Yes, revenue is absolutely a factor in this type of work; however, consistent high levels of revenue are simply a byproduct of doing your job well and with integrity. If you disagree and you believe your job is simply to gain as much revenue at any cost or you simply just don't care, you just want the money, then that's your biggest mistake when working in sales and you are unlikely to have any longevity in this business. Your reputation will catch up with you sooner than you think–a dissatisfied customer will search out everyone they can to alert them of you.

When you're working in sales and aiming to be a leading professional, your mentality needs to reflect a person with authenticity striving to be the best. This is different to what many of you currently believe and are taught. I am sure of this.

Over the years, I have purposefully allowed my revenue and close rate results to speak for themselves as I tested and evolved my style, and you haven't seen me out there hounding other salespeople to tell me their secret to high revenue. I have been constantly asked by employers how I can consistently sell, no matter what the call type. *What's my secret?* I keep getting asked.

I have had co-workers over the years ask me how I can achieve sales levels consistently but then seem to pause for a period and not go past that level. When you're training yourself and developing your skill, you must set targets to measure your results honestly and without outside influence.

This is something that I have believed throughout my entire life. As I wanted to reach higher levels of motor racing and improve my skill, these goals were measured in tenths of a second. I never stop putting these goals out there for me to hit. I would get into a race and set my targets for each race based on lap numbers and where I needed to be. In racing, like in sales, you must employ patience and not move too quickly, because when you do this, you're now racing on uncontrolled emotion, where you're not completely in control of your success. I have failed at this also, particularly in the beginning, and have learned from my mistakes. When I allowed my emotions to control my race, I would experience victory at times but also losses. It became this crazy roller coaster ride where it's either feast or famine.

With no consistency, progress cannot be sustained. You'll burn out and lose any sense of momentum and progression that you are desperately seeking. It was only once I stopped focusing on the results of others, and instead started setting my own personal race goals that were meaningful that I started to see change. Quite often I would purposely qualify near the back of the field to test my mental capability of being able to overcome unknown obstacles that I knew would purposefully trigger high levels of emotion. It was a mental boot camp of sorts, and whilst you may not be able to replicate this same type of training environment to hone your skills, I recommend taking the time outside of work to establish your goals independently of other influences. Once I could master this ability, I would find driving through a race field to be very enjoyable, where most would hate the idea. You must stay laser focused.

I apply this level of focus to my sales goals. Even to this day, I have a notebook in my truck that I reference with weekly goals, results, and longer term aspirational goals. Once I am consistently successful in reaching these revenue goals, I increase the goal further and get clear in my mind on how I will go about achieving it. I adapt and work on new skills to help me reach these aspirational goals. I stay up to date with financial news and market behavior. I am not an economist, but I recognize the importance of broadly understanding what is going on in the world and how this could impact my goals. It is always clearly noticeable to co-workers when I increased my personal revenue goal because they would immediately see the uplift and more importantly see it sustained week in and out. I also begin to be peppered with questions again on what I am doing and how I am getting the numbers.

My success with using this strategy over the years has yielded very high and consistent results no different to how I approach my motor racing training. I have always maintained my ultimate goal of developing a style of sales that has been personally proven in the field over a sustained period of years. I wanted to share how with no experience I was able to start out from the bottom and had learned and developed this style of success by being honest, authentic, and focused. I knew from what I was hearing through training on achieving sales results that it never really sat well with me, and I never really agreed with anything that was being taught. I challenged trainers with questions about what they were teaching, and I decided the best way for me to prove my style was to prove it to myself first, then simply allow my results to speak for themselves. As my results continued to increase year –after year, requests for the "secret ingredient" from co-workers came, along with suggestions that I needed to write this book to share my process with others who were also skeptical or felt at odds with the cookie-cutter training approach.

I can specifically recall a conversation some years back when a manager rang me during the day and said, "I have been reviewing the company numbers for the plumbing department service calls–specifically the revenue and conversion rate on outdoor faucet repairs and pressure regulating valves,"

I simply asked if there was an issue, to which he replied, "Yes, there is, but not with you, with everyone else in the company. I am trying to understand why it is you're able to convert every outdoor faucet repair while usually increasing the job ticket to include extra outdoor faucets and not discount your price while doing this. Most everyone else is not closing these calls or they are closing them at very discounted pricing. In the office we still get calls from customers complaining pricing is too high, but your customers pay our price and actually comment how happy they are when we call them to check in."

He proceeded to ask me for help and if I could explain what I was doing on these calls so he could try and work out how to help everyone else achieve the same results. I obviously gave portions of information, but the simple answer is that most of what I was doing on my calls were my own methods and a style I was still developing. I provided the basis of what I was doing in a customer's home and told him I just simply tell the truth of what is going on in the home regarding their plumbing.

Whilst I shared the crux of what I was doing, I did not share my entire process, as I was still developing this and was not comfortable sharing this more broadly and in an ad hoc manner. I did not see why I should be forthcoming with everything I had been learning and developing, as these were my own methods. Generally speaking, over the years if a person came to me for help, of course I would not turn them away. However, I do not believe in spoon-feeding the answers to them either. This forms a key element of my training as well. I definitely provide information to help them and explain the things I was doing and I would be speaking in a way that if you were genuinely wanting to get better and were giving me the respect of actually listening, then you would be smart enough to read between the lines to piece the information I was giving to you together correctly. I gave advice like I did because when you piece it together for yourself you will also start to incorporate your own thoughts and personality and make the process unique to yourself. If I simply spoon-feed the answers to everyone who asked, they will have no reason to retain the knowledge because they didn't earn it.

Another important point which is a significant contributor to why many have a low close rate is that when they are on a call or talking to a customer regarding a potential sale, ***they are not completely present!***

CHAPTER 11

1% CANCELLATIONS

I have been asked repeatedly how it is I have less than a 1% cancellation rate on the sales I make. They ask how it possibly is that I can easily go against a common belief that the work or goods need an element of urgency when being sold and communicated to the customer, or that everything needs to be completed and given to the customer right now, right as the sale has been agreed to, because if it's not the sale has a high percentage rate of being cancelled when scheduled to be completed in the future.

These concerns of possible cancellation never exist in my mind because these concerns are typical of a salesperson who is the opposite of myself; a salesperson who will routinely use pressure tactics to gain a sale. My customers don't cancel because they feel comfortable and valued from our conversation and the total sales process. They have looked at all the options and are now more than 100 percent confident. There is no room for doubt or second guessing. When you're a true professional you are not lazy–you do your job properly by understanding everything about your customers, products, and services. I will change products very often when challenging a customer on what they think is right, but in doing so I also make sure they are comfortable with their final decision. If you don't and instead you offer the customer only exactly what they are asking for in a rush to close the deal, this will ultimately be the reason you lose the deal and the customer cancels. This is likely to be after your visit when they speak to someone who is not an amateur, not lazy, and not scared to do their job correctly. They were able to present to the customer tangible reasons why the product or service the customer is asking for is actually incorrect. By doing this your job was cancelled immediately because the customer just lost all trust in you.

Never underestimate the power of a customer following their gut instincts and feeling uneasy with moving ahead if you are insincere and outright lazy.

TECHNICAL KNOWLEDGE MATTERS

Traditional training will advise you not to be technical with your customer because it goes over the customer's head and can complicate matters. Now, I disagree with this statement. My advice is that it doesn't matter if you're selling HVAC, plumbing, electrical, cars, real estate, or even clothing. There is a portion of customers out there that absolutely appreciate it when you're technical, when you educate about products and when you share your credible product knowledge with them. Every single customer wants to be educated at some level. Nobody wants to purchase anything blind with no level of confidence and knowledge and without knowing what they're purchasing.

Now, I know this avenue of being technical is not for everybody because a lot of amateurs out there are just lazy and don't actually want to put in the extra effort. When I advise discussing technical aspects with your customer, make sure you talk at the level of the customer. If the customer is a trained engineer–let me tell you right now–if you do not match him or her with the level of respect they deserve as an engineer, you will never close the call. If you are not at a level where you think you can seamlessly talk with an engineer technically about your products or services, then you should invest time and energy into product training right away and educate yourself. Don't be lazy–put in the extra effort to be proficient in everything associated with your line of work.

Almost everyone I have spoken to over the years moans that they can't stand engineers as a customer. I have no issue; in fact, I love it, and find it enjoyable because I make sure I understand every aspect of a product I offer prior to offering it. To the point that I not only want to know all of its selling features, but I also want to understand all of its negative features. If you don't understand the entire facet of the product offering, you will not be ready for any technical objections that will come your way, especially from engineers.

Now, for the person that's not the engineer, you can still cover some technical information to help educate. Make sure you talk on their level—you must assimilate technical terms right after they come out of your mouth with things they would encounter in everyday life. Put items in a descriptive scenario example that they understand while, most importantly, making sure you keep checking in with them. It's very important that you continue to check in with the customers' comprehension of what you're explaining, otherwise you're just going to blow their brain and blow the call because they're going to lose interest. I have witnessed it repeatedly, as many trainers instructing salespeople state that customers don't care about the specifics, they just want you to say you can fix it. My personal interactions with customers and my sales revenues (that's right, actual results, not some theoretical analysis or hypothesis these trainers use) disagree with this perspective.

Of course, customers care. Nobody parts with their hard-earned money without caring about where it's going and why. I've worked for people from all walks of life, and I can without hesitation state that **everybody** cares! Nobody wants to spend their money for no reason, especially when the economy is struggling. Everyone is more anxious about confirming that they are getting value for money. Don't be scared to explain what you're doing during diagnosis of an issue or when evaluating the customer's requests and you'll be surprised at the reactions. A lot of customers will respect you more because in doing so you're demonstrating that you have taken the time to understand everything about what you're in the home to do.

Personally, I get frustrated when I go to buy a car and ask basic questions that the salesperson can't answer. All I think to myself is how arrogant of the salesperson. You want to try to sell me something that you haven't even bothered to learn about yourself? It reeks of laziness and entitlement. There's no way I will ever purchase from that person. I don't give them my business when they haven't answered my simple questions and earned the sale. I will find someone else that has actually earned my business by understanding their product and being able to answer my questions. Stop thinking you have **the right to a sale** just because someone invited you into their home or walked up and asked you a question about a car. **You don't deserve any sale without earning it honestly.** You must work and earn it every day of the week.

I am sure that now you can appreciate the idea that discussing technical product information with the customer is a great and easy way to prove that you have educated yourself. Respect the customer and you have earned the right to the sale. When reviewing technical aspects with the customer, you must be aware in order to know when enough is enough, since as I mentioned above, it is easy to lose the customer if you go too far. If their eyes start to glaze over, you might just want to stop! There is no exact science to managing this situation–you simply need to learn when enough is enough and check in with your customer frequently. As you begin to build experience at reading people's emotions, this will flow with ease. Some good indicators include getting responses to your questions and statements and ensuring you're getting a very easy flow with the back-and-forth conversation. If you are getting good responses and the customer is eager for more information, then move forward. People love to be educated on what they're buying, and this will help you when you present your options because it leads to far less anxiety due to allowing them to have a deeper understanding.

Another negative point to ignoring the opportunity to educate your customer is that they'll try to do this themselves.

Customers think they can be educated from the internet, and a customer educated from the internet is going to likely have a misdiagnosis and need extra time and energy to reverse a mountain of potential misinformation. It's like a calculator–unless you type in the correct terminology and information, you're not going to get the right answer at the end of the search. So, by taking the lead and discussing technical information with the customer, you can quite often debunk a lot of preconceived thoughts that the internet taught a customer. If you are not ready to go ahead and prepare yourself and behave like a true professional, you just straight up missed the opportunity to make sure that the customer is on the right track and in the right frame of mind before you even present any options.

Remember: The right amount of technical insight and discussion with a customer will increase your close rate and sales revenue.

In sales, a lot of the training focuses on managing and overcoming objections in order to gain a sale. The simplest and easiest way to overcome objections is to have all the answers available to you. This sounds obvious, but as obvious as it is, very few grasp this concept and achieve this. It is actually quite astounding how many salespeople out there don't even actually understand the product or service they are selling. It's pure laziness. The fact is that the only reason these salespeople have been making sales is because they focus on getting the low hanging fruit. When that dries up, they will have no other easy option and their sales numbers will reflect this. Any person can make sales from easy calls, but there is no longevity in this approach. You need to be educated and constantly push yourself to learn more. You don't want to be in the business of slashing your prices to overcome lack of education just to stay in the game. Eventually, even this solution will come undone, and you won't be able to sustain your business model. Products change over time, as do the services that businesses offer. Most organizations will support your need to increase your product knowledge and you should take full advantage of these technical training programs.

On various products, it would take me nearly 12 months to be fully educated, prior to me even attempting my first sale of a product or service. This is what your customers deserve. If you do not take the time to educate yourself, you not only run the risk of looking like a fool in front of your customer, but you also have a high chance of losing the sale to someone who has bothered to invest the time to understand the products they are selling. If you think most customers in this day and age have not completed any level of research prior to speaking with you, then you are a complete fool. Why do you think you deserve any of the customers' money and valuable time when you're so lazy you didn't even spend any time of your own to educate yourself and be a true professional in your field.

If you work in an industry that experiences seasonal peaks and troughs, like HVAC for example, you will feel the highs and lows more substantially if you choose to remain uneducated on your product offerings. I know from experience that the seasonality of HVAC has never detrimentally impacted my revenue or conversion rate despite a lower call volume in the off-season. I maintain consistent revenue and conversion when everyone else comes up short because it is simply feast or famine for the uneducated. If you experience feast or famine, that's because the customers that are not purchasing from you are purchasing from salespeople that are professionals who took the time to learn and understand their product offerings, and this knowledge speaks volumes to the customers. Uneducated salespeople struggle with the extra objections coming their way, as the customers are not comfortable enough to make a decision and can observe the lack of confidence and capability of the salesperson in front of them. Meanwhile, the educated salesperson confidently answers and addresses these objections. It bewilders me that if most salespeople fear nothing more than objections during a sales call, then why would you not do everything in your power to be fully prepared? Why would you openly walk into a sales transaction knowing you don't possess the tools to manage these objections about your product or service?

As the saying goes: Knowledge is power!

Ultimately, you're trying to control the direction and outcome of the call, so invest in the power of knowledge and enjoy the benefits of being able to steer your call and be seen as the professional that you're aspiring to be. Without knowledge and product information, revenue is restricted, and you can never be completely confident with what you are selling the customer.

When you have focused on your education and knowledge, you are able to use this to leverage control of your sales call. Never ask questions you don't already know the answers to. You are strategically able to ask questions you know the customer will most likely not have complete answers to, and in doing so this allows you to demonstrate your thorough knowledge of your product or service by expanding on their answers as it relates to them. Through this process, you will earn trust from your customers. Never on any type of sales call should you be asking questions you don't already know the answers to or have a feel for the way in which your customer will respond to your questions. Not doing this correctly will actually make things a lot harder, as it allows the sales call to go in different directions, including potentially into the areas where your lack of education could be exposed in a negative way.

Remember: Educate yourself to guarantee this unpredictability will never happen to you.

NOTES

NOTES

CHAPTER 13

PERSONAL MINDSET

When you're talking with your customers, it's very important to learn to be comfortable. This might sound obvious, and I agree, but just because it's obvious doesn't mean everyone understands what being comfortable actually means.

A lot of people think of themselves as technicians and are not naturally extroverted people. They often enter the world of sales not by choice, making them uncomfortable and out of their natural work environment. It's not a natural transition, if we are all being honest with ourselves. There is absolutely nothing wrong with feeling this way—it is perfectly natural. However, you will not be capable of earning your full potential if you do not overcome this feeling of not being completely comfortable with the term "sales." I want you to be clear here about what I am saying. Do not take this as advice to move away from your technical capabilities and background and start acting the way that the sales trainers will advise you. I believe (and have proven) there is absolutely nothing wrong in using your technical experience to educate your customers. I have spoken at length in this book about how important it is not to shy away from engaging the customer with technical information.

Remember to read the room to determine the amount of technical information and to what detail you provide each customer. When you're not feeling comfortable, your customer will feed off this energy from you, and if they had any anxiety prior to the appointment, it will only increase after they sense your lack of ease in the situation. I often suggest that you find something of interest in the customer's home while you're initially speaking with your customer or take a common point of interest from the initial introduction. At this point it is not about the call itself, but about building the rapport that we have discussed as imperative within this book repeatedly. Your first objective needs to be to focus on getting to know your customer, and your customer getting to know you on a personal level. As soon as you accomplish this you will automatically begin to feel comfortable, setting the tone for the remainder of the call. It allows you to establish all of the other fundamental requirements of a great call. Being comfortable allows you to meet your potential and to extend your call beyond the original reason for being there, and it enables you to be more confident as the call progresses.

An uncomfortable technician will operate with tunnel vision as they stay within their comfort zone. A technician that has not comfortably adopted a sales mindset and remains very focused on dealing with an immediate technical solution only, not factoring in the total sales opportunity, will struggle to ever achieve their potential and be successful. Stop thinking you are doing a good job because you fix repairs and don't get call backs. From a technical standpoint you are doing well, but that is not your only career aspiration. As a technician, work to comfortably accept you're a salesperson with technical knowledge, but still a salesperson. Embrace this, apply your technical knowledge, and step up to the plate with your full potential.

It is important to remember that you can help yourself to start to feel more comfortable in these sales situations by stopping negative thinking to yourself, such as: "*I can't sell. I only know how to fix things.*" All this does is lock you into a very small box of competency and really restricts your capacity for success. When you go into a restaurant do you think the waiter or waitress necessarily knows how to cook anything on their menu? Do you think the chef in the kitchen actually knows how to sell you anything on the menu? They both lack either sales experience or technical experience, depending on their role. One thing I can guarantee though is that the chef who is lacking sales experience would still not just show you one thing on his menu. The chef is going to be proud and show you everything on his menu with the pricing right beside it and ask which of the items on the menu you would like, pointing out the advantages of certain dishes and how they might meet your tastes. The chef is still the chef; however, he has utilized his vast technical capability in a sales setting and created a remarkable experience.

Everything in life has an element of sales, like it or not.

For a technician, I reiterate that once you have established a level of comfortability and know the customer on a personal level, you can then comfortably lean on your technical experience and authentically build a list of items that need repair or replacement to discuss with your customer. By now I am hoping you can see the pattern that sets a successful call and the initial groundwork that needs to be laid in order for all the elements and process steps to be successful. Stop thinking that your technical background defines you, or that you are not capable of expanding your skills into being a successful salesperson. Your technical expertise is actually an advantage. You need to get that negativity out of your mind and don't give the need to sell a second thought. Like the chef, it will come as a natural progression of your skill set when you're confident and comfortable.

Simply continue to follow the process that I have outlined, note all the items you honestly believe, as a technician, need repairing or replacing, but then change one part of your mindset in this moment, which is very important. Just as the technical aspects of a call are important, your customers' time is as valuable as any repair. When you bear this in mind it will help you honestly group together your items that you noted down in order of importance.

Like I said, group everything together by level of importance while also factoring in your customers' time today and future impacts on their time for things not addressed today. Also, always maintain a level of customer engagement during this process. You're actually going to feel very comfortable, as you're allowing your technical experience to guide you just like the chef allowed their technical experience to guide them. Honestly discuss the items you have highlighted and have your customer read your notes for complete clarity and understanding. Now, use your technical experience and consideration of your customers' time as your guide to help you discuss with your customer the reasons behind each of your items as well as the pros and cons of completing and not completing each task. Just be honest and all of your responses will flow naturally. You are now comfortably completing a sales transaction without even allowing the thought of sales to enter your mind. The reason for this occurring is because you're feeling comfortable and you're allowing your expertise to shine through. You have also reinforced your professional capacity with the customer, leaving them with a level of comfort.

When I was describing the example above, you will notice I mentioned everything you noted down as groups to discuss with your customer. I did not use the language you hear from every sales trainer calling them "options to present." Honestly, if you're uncomfortable in sales then the words "options" and "present" will simply trigger your feeling of being uncomfortable. Shake up your terminology to what makes you feel confident and comfortable. I used the words "groups" and "discussing" above, and the customer knows no difference. Try to use terminology that does not represent any form of a sales transaction in your mind to describe this part of the call. This will limit or remove the possibility of you feeling uncomfortable. At the end of the day, it doesn't really matter what terminology you use to describe what you're doing if you know what it means and you're comfortable.

What you will begin to learn as you get more experienced and accept the fact you are as much a salesperson as you are a technician, is that when you complete all the steps of a call as I have outlined in this book, then the sales element of a call is actually not as intimidating as you thought.

Remember: It's not me selling. Truthfully, it is the customer buying.

It is a true level of achievement you can be proud of when your performance is consistent. When call after call, you experience the absolute ease of completing a sale and earning revenue, all while never actually having to feel like you're selling (in the traditional sense) because the customer is buying of their own accord. You are providing guidance to the customer through your interaction and explanations of all the different items you are presenting, but at the end of the day you're now behaving like a professional, and you're never telling the customer, "This is what you need to purchase today—you have no choice here."

Even in very rare instances when there really is only one suitable choice for the customer, you're still completing the exact same steps as any other type of call. You are still going through the process of ensuring the customer feels heard and then guiding them to the best outcome.

Always remember that you're not selling anything. The customer has approached you or invited you into their home because they are ready and wanting to buy from you. If the customer was not ready to buy, they would not be talking to you.

CHAPTER 14

BEING TOLD *NO!*

Stop thinking being told NO and the feeling of rejection is a bad thing.

As all athletes know, the moment you truly see what you're made of is when you feel exhausted and beaten emotionally. That's when we see the true champions that rise–those who have the right stuff mentally to succeed against all odds.

Until you experience feeling exhausted, rejected and mentally beaten, you will never truly be confident in every way. You can, just like everything else in this world, actually condition and train yourself to mentally overcome the empty feeling that arises from being told no and being rejected. When beginners and amateurs are experiencing a low success rate and hearing the word "no" more than "yes," they will start to question themselves internally and become an emotional roller coaster. Emotional roller coasters don't earn revenue and find it difficult to pay the bills. Remember the advice I gave you–to be successful you must remove all doubt and all distractions from your mind to be ready to be successful each and every day.

I am not saying this is an easy thing to condition and train yourself for. This is a behavior you need to experience and practice every day in order to be mentally prepared and focused. Some call it *grit*.

I hope the insight and advice I am giving you in this book makes things easier for you to really understand how you can best prepare your mind for being able to adequately handle rejection and to be able to course correct to get down the right path.

It all starts with working out the positives from being told no and embracing the feeling of rejection. I came to realize this after I was already given these negative responses over a hundred times at least.

At this point I felt all the emotions that came with being told no. Being angry and questioning myself as well as companies and individuals is what came to the forefront of my emotions in the beginning. It is easy to shift the excuses to others and what you feel are their shortcomings.

All of this came about prior to me ever entering the world of sales.

Whoever thought that being a race car driver required you to be a full-time salesperson? I started motor racing in Australia and had exciting opportunities to move to America to continue racing. As I progressed, I accepted commercial sponsorship money that was needed to be able to continue and compete at a higher level. I had absolutely no commercial business contacts I could turn to and was thinking how on earth could I make this happen? I didn't necessarily see this next step as a move into sales. That was a big mistake on my part, and I learned the hard way. After spending such a significant amount of time researching every company worldwide that I thought were a fit commercially and could genuinely make money from my motor racing, I would either call, mail, or email each of them one by one.

On a side note, always reply to anyone that sends you a request. Even if your answer is no. They took the time to send you a request, so be a respectful person and reply.

The replies I received for the most part were a flat-out "no." They would give me one reason or another, and sometimes no reason at all. Some were decent and gave small bits of advice and I wrote a respectful and thankful reply to every single negative response I got. I stayed focused even while being angry and disappointed inside and continued company after company, still turning up the same results. A long way into this process I then started seeing companies whom I contacted turning up as sponsors on major teams in America. At first this made me even angrier, but then I realized the mental grit and perseverance I developed stopped me feeling angry. I asked an unimaginable number of questions about everything during this entire time and started to find the positives in every response I was rejected in. To the companies that wound up on other race cars, I felt reassured that my research was 100 percent correct. None of these companies had anything to do with motorsport prior to my contact.

I then started to see everything I was doing was sales and that I had approached most of it all wrong. Searching for commercial sponsorship was cold calling, which I believe is the hardest type of sales you could be exposed to. I had unknowingly found myself in the equivalent of cold calling and door to door sales. I dropped myself right in the deep end of sales and to add to the craziness I was not attempting to close a sale of a few hundred or a few thousand dollars like an average cold call. Instead, I was attempting to close sales deals of hundreds of thousands of dollars, if not millions, and I hadn't truly given it a second thought. In the professional world of sales, the majority of the best salespeople would not have the guts or confidence to do this, simply because they know there is a high percentage rate of failure to close deals of this magnitude, especially with no introduction or relationship with the other party involved.

They will question if they can mentally cope with the rejection and come out on the other side more confident than when they started. Confidence is the biggest key to high performance in sales. Most will never willingly allow it to be questioned or challenged. But remember: If an athlete never questions their own performance by increasing challenges and possibly losing, they never truly become worthy of the highest ranks of achievement in their field and a true, sustainable champion to the best of their abilities.

All current salespeople that think they are great and have no problem telling you how great they are, will just be a flash in the pan. Hot for a second then gone and forgotten about. They will never be a high performing, sustained achiever, because they never truly trained themselves mentally to deal with being told no and the feeling of rejection. Maybe they have had luck on their side, or an in-demand product or no real competition. The fact remains they have never been tested and have never had to be hungry for the sale or deal while coming back from rejection. No one can truly outline their ability honestly without experiencing rejection and failure, without diving in the deep and being able to rise back to the top. If anyone tells you differently, I would seriously doubt them or the circumstances they operate within.

Experience is the most powerful tool for learning anything. A baby isn't born knowing how to walk–they must be taught and experience taking steps, falling, and getting back up again. A baby must experience success and failure. They must fall over and over before they truly get it right. Imagine if we just stopped getting up as young children? We would all still be crawling all over the place, never actually developing and evolving. Even at our earliest challenge in life we must fall on our ass over and over to literally rise and stand on our own two feet.

Do not overcomplicate things!

I dealt with and experienced the feeling of rejection so many times I lost count during this period. It trained me mentally, and I honestly trained myself without realizing. For me, I was focused enough mentally to never stop or question my goals in the first place. Years of rejection can generally send a person spiraling out of control and questioning their abilities and what they are trying to achieve. That is very real, and the biggest fear experienced by most people. That's the first big step to overcome.

Remember: Don't allow fear of the unknown to control you. Master it, face it head on, and be prepared for any outcome with complete unwavering confidence and control in the situation!

This is the moment I found out what I was truly capable of and how determined I am as a person inside. You must remember that the feeling of rejection and failure, just like anything else you train for in life, must be experienced over and over for you to learn how to confidentially deal with it mentally and not allow it to control your ability to be highly successful. Eventually it made me able to accept any rejection without feeling any level of anger and without questioning myself or what I was doing confidentially.

You must go through the dark to get to the light. Every path you chose is a path worth taking with no regrets when you control your emotions confidently and positively.

Others that have joined me on a sales call to observe often mentioned that it was difficult to work out what I was thinking during the call. And by that, I mean it was difficult for them to determine what I was thinking about the call, the customer, and my end goal for the sale. I guess you could call this a good poker face. One example I recall is when the person told me after I closed the sale how they had no idea how I just closed the call. This was from a guy who will close consistent sales worth millions per year. He commented how he would never have closed the sale, and that he had no idea how the sale went ahead given the number of objections I was given by the customer from the moment we met at the door. Through the entire call I overcame each objection, to even on occasion confidently not addressing an objection if I didn't want to. He was bewildered by my approach. I was running the call in a style he had never seen before.

This isn't the first time I have received this type of feedback about my style from a fellow salesperson. On another occasion, when joined by another individual capable of closing millions per year in sales, I was described in the exact same way–calm and unfazed by the possible objections and hurdles being put up by the customer. He said, "It is crazy, while you are eager to close sales calls, you walk in and seem as if to not really care one way or another if you close the sale. But you will close the sale *and* with upgrades, without even trying."

I want to close each call as much as the next person. And I obviously like being successful and in control of my own success. I put as much effort in as the next person–probably more. The difference is as I mentioned: I have trained myself through experiencing rejection to remain controlled through a sales call to reign in all emotions, regardless of when a customer says yes or no. I will not become an emotional roller coaster and I will remain neutral (and still professional and engaging with the customer) one way or another. I will always remain in control and be direct, which will, even with the toughest personality in a customer, eventually allow you to guide the call exactly how you want with the outcome you want. This level of controlled emotion is strange to some but allows control of the situation and ensures you don't end up with an outcome driven by your emotions and not by fact, experience and the customers emotions.

To become successful, you must master being told no AND control your emotive response to the situation. I cannot stress this enough!

I have had many customers greet me at the door with, "I don't even know why you're here. I didn't make the appointment, my partner did, and I want to be clear I am not buying anything, OK."

Unlike most salespeople who are already now mentally writing off the call and working out how to quickly get out, I actually love these customers, as right at that moment I actually have complete control of the call even though they may think the opposite. Remember: You can control the outcome. The main reason I love these types of calls though is that the customer has shown you right away they are a strong-willed, emotional person. They are presenting an elevated level of emotion right at the door. They are already an emotional roller coaster allowing themselves to be easily read. Now, if you are confident in controlling your emotions you can have control of this type of customer situation immediately. If you are unable to completely control your emotions, then this call potentially will be very difficult and could result in a waste of time for you. If you remain in complete control of your emotions, seamlessly responding to each of the customer's challenging statements with the correct level of confident emotion control, they will then become confused as to why their strategy–which works every time–has not rattled you at all. Through this, you will actually instill confidence in the customer and start to gain their trust. You can see it in their eyes and body language as a result of them being an emotional person on an emotional roller coaster. In a way, by being so in control of your own emotions and responses, you have been rejecting their every statement of not being interested in what you have to offer just by being present on the sales call.

Because they are not trained to deal with rejection you always had complete control. It's very fulfilling professionally to experience this type of success on a call. That's why I enjoy the challenge these types of calls offer.

Let me reiterate: *You need to stop thinking being told NO and the feeling of rejection are terrible things.*

Remember: As all athletes know, the time you truly see what you're made of is when you feel exhausted and beaten emotionally. That's when we see the true champions rise that will succeed and who have the stuff mentally to succeed against all odds.

CHAPTER 15

STAYING ON TARGET

I don't want every customer. I only want my customers. It's my choice who I work for.

Thinking that you want every single customer is a very large mistake many make in business and in sales. When you start out you have a clear mindset of who your customers are. Never forget this mindset. Marketers call it "customer segmentation," but to dial it down into simple terms, you want the right customer that is going to allow you to maximize your profit because the cost to convert the sale is efficient and optimized. Do not allow yourself to enter into any agreement with a customer you do not want. When this happens, you have lost control and confidence in yourself. This happens very often when a salesperson becomes desperate to meet a minimum expected sales revenue goal, for example. You will start down a very slippery slope that can be extremely hard to come back from. What will happen is that you will start to see increases in your cost of operating. This can come from call backs, decreased profit margins and poor reviews. This small amount is not your true worth; it's simply because you're allowing yourself to work for the wrong customer. The further you go down this slope the more you will begin to question everything you previously knew to be right and what had worked for you consistently. You will start to lose sight of your business goals and will stop growing to the levels of revenue you deserve.

Another sports analogy for you: quarterbacks commonly have this issue. They can be superstars known for their impressive down field passing and confidence through any defense to score touchdowns time after time. You see it in star batters in baseball also, where they're capable of home runs over and over. However, the minute the quarterback falls on a couple of bad passes, which can grow into a series of bad passes, the quarterback will begin to lose sight of the player they deserve to be. They will start looking for low hanging fruit and pass rush, throw short and throw low risk passes at best. This strategy will somewhat curb the ball from being intercepted and make them feel a little more comfortable. They might even win a few games. The longer they keep doing this though, they will lose the confidence to access their full potential and skill to make the long passes down the field and to make the confident passes through the defense which score consistent quality touchdowns and win big games. Very rarely can they come back from this, and as a result, they lose monetary value for taking the comfortable approach and end up being traded or dropped. The same fate applies to the star batter. They start getting caught out or miss the ball and strike out. Then they start accepting first base as a result.

The longer they become comfortable with first base, the more at risk they will be of having the same unfortunate fate as the quarterback and end up traded or dropped. They have the ability to hit home runs and that is why they were employed. That is their true ability and worth. On both examples they lost sight of their personal goals and chose to accept being comfortable instead of being who they were meant to be: *real champions*. When they faulted, they made the mistake of not examining themselves internally and evolving their training to stay successful. They refused to be brutally honest with themselves like no one else could be. "Just enough" became their benchmark, rather than being the best. In this competitive world, just enough will not cut it.

When you as a salesperson start to experience not closing sales–and these are in succession–before you start changing up everything to try and close the next sale, scrambling for anything that comes your way, first sit back and examine the previous calls. Where did the call go south and fail?

Remember:

- Get your emotions in check

- Clear your mind of other distractions

- Be honest with yourself about your performance

- Identify opportunities for growth (skill, experience, style, customer service)

And importantly, ask yourself:

Was this customer your target customer? Was the customer wanting from you something you were not willing or able to provide? Whether that be to discount your price or to work at a workmanship standard you believe unacceptable, don't go changing everything just to get the sale. Be brave enough to walk away and simply explain to the customer you are not the right person or company to complete the work or service the customer is requesting and give suggestions on whom they could possibly call to help them. I never give specific details as a recommendation because if the customer has a bad experience with your recommendation you could end up being blamed for the bad experience. If you start changing your price or workmanship because you're not brave enough to walk away, soon you will lose the confidence to operate at the high level you deserve. If you examine the call failure and break down your performance to understand what has occurred, then learn from it and evolve for the next call. Do not take the low hanging fruit to feel comfortable–this will stop you from reaching the high levels of sales you deserve whilst stopping your growth and company growth. There is nothing wrong with feeling a little uncomfortable, as it will spur you on to continued growth and higher success in sales.

This approach is no different to companies directing their marketing at a target market, which is the customer segmentation that I mentioned earlier. No successful company is out there trying to get every customer type and location within their market space. Everyone that is successful will always remain completely focused on their target market, without compromise. This is because they know their product offer, understand the customer, and have spent a lot of time, money and energy working on how to best capitalize on this market share. Of course, this target market will potentially evolve and change from time to time. Never lose sight of the simple fact that your customers are your target market that aligns with your organization's goals also. You cannot be off trying to build a different customer base, as it's simply not efficient for your organization and the professional tools you have been given and developed will be of little use to you in being successful. Be brave and walk away if they are not the right customer and don't change yourself to make a sale. You do not need every single customer out there in the world. *Work smarter!*

Close your calls in your target market and you will enjoy what you do in the world of sales AND be successful. If you allow yourself to enter a customer market segment that is not your target you will quickly, just like the quarterback and baseball player, grow frustrated, lose value, and ultimately never achieve the goals you deserve.

Remember: Work smarter making profits and not harder chasing—you will end up growing frustrated without profits!

NOTES

NOTES

NOTES

CHAPTER 16

HAVING A FLUID APPROACH

An adjustable personality will lead to success in sales.

Over the years the world has progressively adjusted in terms of financial and demographic locations. As a result, this has created a diverse mix of personality types across all market segmentations. Whereas in the past if you focused on a particular market segmentation you were confident in knowing the personality type you would be interacting with on a daily basis. As it is today there is no real guarantee of anything when it comes to the type of personality you will be encountering on a daily basis. Rather than becoming frustrated by this and creating your own roadblocks for not closing the sale, remain positive, educate yourself and develop new skills.

This can sometimes be hard for some, but it's extremely important to develop the ability to adjust your personality to increase the amount of success you can experience. All customers have different personalities. If our customers all have different personalities and are not all cookie-cutter, then why do you think giving a cookie-cutter approach to every customer will work to gain a sale? During a sales call you have probably been taught that you must mirror your customer's personality to be successful. I prefer to say rather than mirror your customer's personality, simply adjust your own personality to one that is compatible with your customer's personality. Sometimes mirroring your customer's personality can have a negative effect on the sales call because it creates a personality clash. On some occasions you will be dealing with more than one person, like a couple for example. An amateur mistake is to discover the personality of one of the partners that fits with your own and direct most of your presentation to them.

When you're not trained to have the ability to adjust your personality you will find yourself making this mistake without even knowing. As a result, you often will not close this call because you excluded one person from the presentation. This then became a huge roadblock stopping you from getting the sale. An example is one person might be very analytical as a purchaser, whilst the other person is an emotional purchaser. You must be sure to engage each in their own way. You will need to give almost two separate presentations to be sure you will stand out and be successful with the sale. Generally, I recommend engaging the analytical person first while checking in with brief details to the emotional purchaser. Continue this process until you see the analytical purchaser satisfied and comfortable. It is far easier to lose the sale if the analytical person is not comfortable, as they will give off an uncomfortable negative feeling which the emotional purchaser will feed off of and emotionally and subconsciously start feeling the same way. By keeping the emotional purchaser engaged with brief details, the moment the analytical purchaser feels comfortable and confident in the decision to purchase, the emotional purchaser will feed off that positive emotion and feel the same way. Once you notice this is happening, start presenting equally to both, giving a recap of the highlights you want to point out, assuring both customers are clear and comfortable with the offering and ready to move forward with the sale. This will result in successfully closing the sale.

Here is another scenario that demonstrates the importance of gaining the ability to adjust your personality. Imagine that, when presenting to one person and they are almost ready to proceed with the purchase, another person the customer knows then walks into the home. Be it a friend, parent, or partner, it doesn't really matter. This new person will be curious to know what's going on and will quite often insert their own advice and experiences into the situation. Immediately your customer will be looking to this person subconsciously for reassurance that they are making the right decision. You must address this concern your customer is feeling immediately by quickly identifying the visitor's personality and adjusting your personality to suit as needed while confidently explaining the current issues that are being experienced and moving to the advantages with the purchase or work to be completed. As long as you have made this additional person feel comfortable, your customer is again ready to purchase.

It sounds frustrating to have someone who is not the purchaser have such an impact on your sales call, but it is a common occurrence, and you need to have a game plan in place so you do not become flustered and can remain focused. If you don't learn how to adjust your personality so you can manage this scenario quickly and seamlessly, your likelihood of closing a sale will decrease rapidly for every minute that goes by where this additional person has not been made to feel comfortable.

Remember: Learning to adjust your personality will increase your conversion rate!

CHAPTER 17

WORK SMARTER, NOT HARDER

I mentioned this previously when I outlined the steps on how to run a successful call, but I want to circle back to this particular step because it's extremely important and can be overlooked entirely to the detriment of everyone involved.

Whether you are called out to a customer's home or a customer comes into your place of work, and whether it's buying a car, buying a house, or buying clothing, that initial want, concern, or issue that the customer has is the **most important thing** to that customer at that given point in time. If you go out to the house for example, and you're there to look at a dripping tap, or why the thermostat won't work, or why a light switch doesn't work, you must spend more time on that particular item before you begin to talk about anything else that you noticed in the home and took notes on. If you don't spend a larger amount of time and focus addressing the initial concern that the customer has, you're not going to be seen as trustworthy, or as being very genuine. And, quite honestly, you're probably not being very genuine. The chances of you closing this sale are diminishing by the minute. A customer will begin to trust you more and more no matter how small the task if you can explain the issue and remedy it using more than one-word responses. Make sure you take the long way around, apportioning an appropriate amount of time explaining the reasons for the issue at hand and the recommended remedy.

Many sales trainers will tell you not to try and educate a customer with technical information as it will make them feel uncomfortable. They also believe an educated customer will potentially come up with questions and objections during this process that could cause you to stumble. Personally, you should take offense that this style of training assumes you're not up to managing the questions that could come from being professional and technical with your observations.

I would ask you to genuinely make sure you help educate customers that show interest, especially if you see that they are of an analytical mind. They will greatly appreciate you engaging them at an appropriate level, and you will gain their trust immediately. You must always talk to a customer at their level. If the customer is not analytically inclined, you still need to take the long way around so that they can see you are putting in the effort and taking care to solve their initial concern and not trying to just upsell them or gouge them but are simply focused on solving their issue. It doesn't matter if you end up spending an hour on this initial concern and you think you should have only spent 10 minutes—I can tell you right now that when you get the ratio correct, moving to any extra items that you're suggesting to the ticket will flow seamlessly. It will be quite an easy conversation now to include extra items.

I have lost count how many times I have been out looking at issues to do with plumbing and, yes, on nearly every one of these calls the plumbing item was broken, however, there is almost always another reason that contributed to the plumbing issue the customer was experiencing. If I follow my process and give the correct amount of time to the initial issue, moving the call toward including extra items like water treatment is seamless. At this point the customer is very eager to get everything solved and to avoid any further issues with their home and water quality. If you're not earning the right to explain this to a customer and demonstrate potential issues, then why do you think you're actually helping the customer? All you're doing is walking out of there with a few hundred dollars in an approved plumbing repair when you could be walking out of there with thousands.

Being capable of following this process will have you converting your sales potential every time. I can tell you straight up from actual experience when running plumbing calls, I would upsell a water filtration system on the majority of sales. Now, whether it be a small treatment option or a full-scale, top of the line system, customers always purchased an extra treatment system because I earned their trust. Ideally, they want to resolve all possible issues with one single call. The customer arrives at this decision on their own because you successfully educated them. Again, that's right–don't be scared to educate a customer.

Remember: An informed person will purchase at a much higher rate than an uninformed person.

So, why is everyone too scared to talk to the customer straight? Go ahead, try it! You will have success, and it does not matter how small the task is. It does not matter if you're out there to do a free flush on a water heater. You're given an opportunity to create revenue for yourself and for your business, but you need to take the plunge and put yourself out there. An example of building value from a small opportunity is an offer that is made available by most service companies both domestically and internationally–the discounted water heater flush. These are referred to as *loss leaders*. On these calls you will see the difference between an amateur and a professional. An amateur is inspecting or just straight up dumping water down the drain and moving on to the next call, not respecting the sales opportunity you have actually been given. Most technicians and amateurs out there can't stand running these types of calls and will moan about it to everyone that will listen. I am proof that you can run that call and you can watch your revenue skyrocket by simply just doing your job, doing what's right by the customer, and asking them straight up when you get into the home exactly what their expectations and requirements for the coupon service call are in order to make them open up honestly. This will lead to them expanding on any issues within their home.

Also, ask questions at this time. This will aid you in your broader goal of driving the optimized revenue outcome. I can confirm to you from experience that customers will tell you, "I'm not paying you to tell me what I want to hear so I think I feel better. I'm paying you to come out here and tell me exactly what's wrong in my water heater." Listen to your customers and take the time to understand their concerns and points of view. Do this and you will see success because, as we all know, water heaters don't last forever.

Listen, there will still be 1% of these types of calls where they are in great shape because they've been serviced every year, and the customer is just using a free coupon offer to keep their appliance in that level of working order. I can tell you right now though that there are components on that water heater, and I'm not going to go into it because this is not a plumbing book, that will need replacing periodically. There is significant pipework attached to a water heater. In fact, the entire plumbing system is attached to this water heater and if you do your job properly you will see these revenue opportunities because you will uncover issues in this type of house every day of the week.

Remember: Stop moaning about running your water heater tune up call and get after it. An opportunity is an opportunity. Your attitude and approach define what your outcome will be.

Get your head in the game, smile, and run these tune ups and convert these calls into thousands of dollars.

OPTIMIZE YOUR CALL TIME

Every and any type of potential sale has no time limit ever.

I will begin by reiterating the section in my steps on how to run a call. "Do not answer your phone" is a simple thing that will make a big difference. To expand on this, you must not be thinking about any other past or potential call than the one you're on. You will give the current customer your complete attention, with no pre-set time limit, ever. No customer other than the customer in front of you is of any importance.

Many salespeople will shy away from running free estimate calls, as they are notoriously perceived for being time-wasting and are said to (at best) have an average close rate of 20-30 percent. In other words, they have all the hallmarks of a call that is not going to contribute to your success or goal of revenue increase. "Statistically, you have to run a higher volume of these calls," you're told, "expect the low close rate and revenue because you're operating on the law of averages, meaning if you run a high volume, you could potentially achieve enough sales to hopefully satisfy your minimum sales goals."

When did aiming for the minimum become acceptable? This is a lie and an excuse that people tell themselves because they actually do not have the internal drive and desire to learn more, to buck this trend and be the exception. Many sales people simply want the easy money and are too lazy to learn and develop the skills to be truly professional. Think about the ebb and flow of the economy for just a minute. Do you think these salespeople will be able to have success when the economy is in a downcycle? They will be out of a job because they have only maintained sales in easy situations, where the opportunity fell at their feet. They lack the tenacity, grit, and skills to be able to remain an asset despite the change of economic conditions. Unfortunately, on these call types, an amateur salesperson's biggest hurdle is listening to the advice from their peers, who tell them these calls are no good, so don't bother trying and just get in and out as quickly as possible. That's the same advice I was given when I was starting out. I, however, made a conscious decision that I would not accept that advice. Let's just entertain for a second that you do in fact blow through the call quickly, eager to get to the next one (if it exists). What if that call is also a free estimate? And the one after that? Then what?

For me, it makes absolutely no difference if I am on a call as a referral, breakdown, or even a free estimate. I want my close rate and revenue to be the highest possible. If you are truly a professional, you should not be constricted by simple beliefs that something is not achievable. I always have the strong belief that no one can ever help the customer the way I can, and my job is to make sure I do the best I can possibly do to win the job and secure the revenue. This is the difference between a flash-in-the-pan salesperson and a true professional. The professional believes in their capabilities, and this belief will naturally shine through without ever having to think about it.

Remember: Find the genuine internal motivator that drives you to succeed and embrace it with every part of your being, so that it simply becomes an extension of you on every sales call.

When it came to free estimate calls, I decided I would try something completely different. I would give the same unlimited amount of time and attention to the call and customer as I would give to a referral. My instincts told me that it was worth investing the time to see if this could generate a higher revenue and close rate. Why do we think we should be operating on the law of averages, especially on estimates, which in the industry these days are generally paid leads from a lead generation website? For an organization such as the one you work for, if they are paying for these leads, especially in the quiet times, the act of you burning through these calls and not giving them the time they actually require is also draining your company of resources and they will soon enough realize this. *How is this smart?* If these are paid leads, wouldn't it be more prudent to actually make sure you get the most out of this investment? I make sure any investment made to generate free estimate calls is an investment with results.

Given the right time, energy and focus, these calls can be just as successful. I don't operate on the pathetic excuse that these calls are dead before you even get to the front door. I operate on the thought process that every call has the same equal level of importance. Customers will routinely comment how they have never had a person in their home to provide an estimate that was as thorough and focused on the job. Be mindful that the customer is in the process of getting estimates–most customers in the U.S., for example, will typically get three estimates before considering a decision, so you need to stand out through your service and expertise. You will experience though, when providing the right amount of time and energy on estimates, that the customers feel more than comfortable giving approval and proceeding without worrying about further estimates. The attention I give when on these free estimates (and if you do the same) will have you so surprised you won't even need to ask the customer to show their previous estimates to you if you're not the first person in their home. They will most likely offer up this information prior to you even presenting your pricing. The reason that this occurs is because you are the only person behaving as a true professional, and in the mind of the customer, you're not just a salesperson anymore–you are viewed as a trusted friend. The customer feels more respected and is therefore more likely to be transparent with the information they have and what they are thinking with regards to selecting a company to do business with. Just by following my process on estimates, not only did my close rate increase dramatically, but I also experienced a steep increase in my revenue. I was now able to build up from the original estimate and increase the value by including extra items the customer may have expressed a desire for in addition to the original scope of work.

Treat this call as no different to any other demand call. You need to ask questions relating to the purpose of the estimate and desired results once they have purchased the item they are requesting the estimate for. Very often during this discussion you can realize that for the customer to be truly satisfied with their purchase there might be something else that needs to be installed or purchased to enhance the benefits they require. This is when you should not be scared to start providing more authentic education, providing that extra level of product or service information that we have discussed throughout this book. Showing the customer the product options that you have determined will achieve and exceed the customers' expectations. This will also demonstrate your industry experience and knowledge. Remember that this builds momentum and credibility in your sales call. Provide all customers with the same level of respect. I find it funny (and honestly an easy win) when I am on a free estimate call and I see the previous joker doing the same as everyone else and burning through calls, running more than double the amount I run and making less revenue than I do.

On some calls, even after doing everything correctly, you may not have received approval. This can be for any number of reasons, and many of which are out of your control. Do not stress and don't become anxious or pushy. Be confident that you have covered everything within your control, and that no one else is capable of everything you have just done in the customer's home on this free estimate. My advice prior to leaving is to simply open your tablet or your calendar and simply ask the customer what their preferred date and time would be for you to check back in with them to answer any new questions that they have at that time. It's very important, once making this statement, that you do not say another word. Be patient and wait for the customer's response. It's important that the customer is the one who chooses the date and time for you to call them back or to come back to their home, because at this moment they are now psychologically not only making a commitment to you, but also to themselves regarding this appointment.

Respond to the customer with confirmation of the agreed date and time, that you look forward to speaking with them and that they should not hesitate to reach out with any questions that they may think of between now and that agreed time. If you're getting a less than favorable response, then you are still performing like an amateur and are not yet a professional earning the customer's trust. This is particularly important when your goal is increasing your close rate and revenue. The call is not over, so don't be despondent if you're doing more follow-ups. I routinely schedule follow-up calls that will end in a successful sale. I have even on occasion suggested to customers to go ahead and get more estimates, because when I call the customer back, I am interested to hear what they have to say regarding their comparative experience. They will usually be a little surprised at this approach, but let's be honest: if they're going to get estimates anyway, there is no point in shying away from it. You may as well bring it up yourself and be confident in doing so. Even consider making it lighthearted with a little humor. By not shying away and taking this confident approach, you build extra credibility between the customer and yourself.

The experience you are creating will shadow the amateurish approaches from other salespeople they will interact with.

When you remain confident and professional, it makes the process a pleasurable, memorable experience. The customer remembers this experience once you leave, which solidifies the customers' trust in you. The majority of times I have completed my calls in this manner, the customer will reach out to me earlier than our scheduled time on their own accord and give approval to proceed with the work. Remain authentic and professional on every call, remain confident and do not be scared to be compared to other salespeople in your industry. Be honest with the customers' true needs and you will succeed and increase your close rate and revenue substantially.

Remember: You must always maintain the internal belief that, "No one can ever help the customer the way I can."

It is about time you became a real professional and started working smarter and not harder.

It goes without saying that you should be spending an appropriate amount of time on demand calls, as these are your big-ticket calls that you want to really maximize. As a guide, I can confidently say from my experience that anyone completing demand calls in under two or three hours is burning through the call. You're not maximizing your earning potential when you're burning through a call. When you approach these calls with the process I have outlined in this book, then you are going to see a shift in your call metrics. You are going to be running a smaller number of calls but with increased revenue. Aka: smarter, not harder!

There is no reason you should be rushing in and out of these calls after all, rushing a recommendation for a quick repair without properly reviewing the root cause of the failure is substantially wasting your business marketing dollars whilst operating in a counterproductive manner for your own sales success. You are directly causing your overheads to balloon out of control, systematically destroying your profit margins and pricing yourself out of competition. Ultimately, there is no positive outcome that results from burning through any type of call and operating with a low close rate. By not fixing the root cause of the part or service failure, you will be causing your customer to waste more time in the future when it inevitably breaks again, and your chances of the customer calling you back a second time are frankly unlikely because of how disappointed they are in having the same issue occur after you assured them everything was fixed. You just burnt through a call, lost repeat business, and destroyed your reputation.

This can all be alleviated by following this advice:

Take your time, diagnose correctly, be a professional and build a sustainable business.

Remember: There is so much at stake when you burn through any type of call, so STOP doing it and enjoy a higher close rate and higher revenue.

NOTES

NOTES

NOTES

CHAPTER 19

OPTIONS, PRESENTATION AND LAYOUT

There has been a lot of discussion in sales as to what the best practice is to lay out your options when presenting them to a customer. I am sure you have all heard the tried and tested formula of starting with your most expensive, as it causes the customer to think that anything below this will be more economical and comfortable by comparison. It makes selling your middle option that much easier because as the customer moves further into the discussion, the pricing goes down progressively and not up.

This tactic is designed to confront your customer with the sticker shock of the expensive option that you're not really trying to sell but is being used to establish a high and effective price conditioner so that the customer is feeling much more comfortable to purchase your mid-range options rather than your low-end options. In the service industry we have all been taught similar strategies to sell the middle option or options, depending on how many you have written.

Let me share my journey of what I have discovered over the years regarding this strategy, particularly in the service industry. In the beginning I would write my options on a yellow legal pad. I was writing them side by side in column format on one page. I would start with the cheapest option, moving across to the highest-priced option. Now for me personally, I wrote the cheapest on the right-hand side of the page with highest option on the left. Then when I presented, I presented left to right. I initially started out with what I was told in training, that you need to start with your highest price option and end with your cheapest. My customers would choose my middle option most of the time, but sometimes my cheapest. What I wanted to achieve was a shift that would result in more customers purchasing from the highest price options. My goal, as it has always been, was to grow my revenue, and without this successful shift, I was not going to be able to make this possible. I decided to switch up my approach to see what results I could generate. Becoming curious and not accepting the status quo is something that, by now, you should see is the approach I have to everything.

Now, when writing in a column-style format on a legal pad, I also noticed that you really did waste a lot of space on the paper. So, I began writing them one on top of the other on a single page. I wrote my cheapest at the bottom of the page with highest priced at the top of the page. Then to switch things up further, I was also not showing any pricing initially. I would present my options without pricing to the customer, knowingly presenting from my cheapest to my most expensive. Once the customer gave the indication of what they preferably wanted, I then put the pricing next to each option. In doing so I would reiterate each of the options from cheapest to most expensive with the customer and allow them to guide their preference. This is the complete opposite manner to how you will be taught in your sales training, but in employing this approach I was actually selling more of the mid-to-high range packages. I also reintroduced pricing at times to pressure test my presentation techniques and ensure I am optimizing my engagement with various customer segments. I concluded I did not believe in the notion of needing to use any type of pricing strategy in my presentation to achieve the best outcome for all involved. I also often presented my options with no logical flow, and I can honestly say doing this and adding the pricing back in had no negative impact on my sales or conversion rate results. I realized that my higher option sales success was unaffected by the way in which I was presenting my options layout. Ultimately, it was more affected by how I was running my calls. It goes back to comfortably earning a customer's trust and approval through this method of running a successful sales call. It truly makes no difference how expensive an option is if it is honestly the best option for the customer. They will also come to the same conclusion and want to proceed with that option. To reiterate, remember that I confirmed, through my trials, that the customer will purchase with emotion every time, with price being a small consideration in most transactions.

Following this, I thought I would change things up again, and on some calls, I even wrote my options on paper I ripped out of my note pad, so it did not look professional at all in order to test the presentation layout theory. It made no ultimate difference to the sale. I confirmed the customer will not object to your options in any layout if you complete the call correctly prior to presentation. As I have mentioned to people over the years that have genuinely asked for help, that prior to you ever putting your options together, through your discussions and interactions with your customer, you should already know everything the customer wants, needs, and would like to include prior to ever writing an option. Talk to the customer as you build the options—it builds trust and demonstrates transparency in the process. This gives you the opportunity to discuss and emotionally sell the option you're wanting to sell to your customer well ahead of even presenting them. This is far more important than any format or way in which you present, so stop stressing about your options layout and presentation. I am highlighting here, especially to those starting out in this field and who are so nervous about writing options, that the layout and the presentation are not what will make or break your sale.

Don't go too crazy with options, as it simply becomes over whelming for the customer. I have heard anywhere from three to eight options, if needed, are suitable. From my personal experience I would advise that you should routinely aim for three to four written options. As you guide the customer to your preferred option verbally prior to presenting, you will now know confidently which additional items could likely be incorporated successfully. You're also learning which items should not be included, as the customer is not interested, and so it is not worth risking the success of your call focusing on these items.

As a tip: sometimes, when estimating multiple trade disciplines, you should consider putting the separate trade disciplines on separate option pages so you don't overwhelm the customer. By sticking to just three or four options you will get more approvals to proceed because you are no longer confusing or overwhelming your customer.

A great example of refining your product option and still achieving financial success is the IN 'N'OUT Burger brand. If you are familiar with this fast-food chain, you will know that there are limited options to choose from on their menu, with each being carefully refined so as not to overwhelm the customer. In most cases, this results in "add-ons" also being included, increasing the overall ticket value. Judging by their huge popularity and turnover, this strategic approach to their menu is very well received by customers.

Remember: Don't let creating options induce anxiety or stress. It is a minor part of every call when a call is executed correctly from the start.

CHAPTER 20

LASER FOCUSED

Focus on what's in front of you only!

It's time to respect and appreciate the call that you're on and stop looking ahead to the next call. You'll never regret it.

In fact, you will enjoy every day that you go to work, as well as revenue and success that you never thought possible.

Now, to give an example: Imagine you go to run a basic furnace tune up. Many technicians will complain about these types of calls. They just see too much work for potentially not enough revenue. Fact is, everybody wants to run the breakdowns on the 20+ year old equipment, but the majority of calls will come from coupons.

Very rarely is someone going to ring you up and say, "Hey by the way, come to my house. I want to spend $50,000 on a HVAC system." I mean, when these types of calls come in, they are great. You know you are likely to be successful on a big-dollar ticket. But the fact remains that you're going to get a tremendous number of calls where people want you to come out and just do a tune-up. They want you to come out to the house and be honest, and the simple reality is that that is all you need to do in order to be successful and convert a furnace tune-up into a larger sale.

Demonstrate to the customer what needs to be repaired but remain honest. More often than not, if that equipment really is in bad shape and needs repair, you will see the customer prompt you to provide them with options and grant you the approval to go from a coupon-based tune-up to a larger, more expensive repair or replacement option. This increase in revenue will only become a reality if you stay focused, confident, and upbeat about the possibilities in front of you. This will put you in the best position to optimize the steps I have outlined in this book.

I have developed these steps for you to follow on your calls and to keep coming back to reference and build your confidence and ability in areas of a sales call. You must spend the same amount of time and give every customer the same effort and respect whether you're out there to do a coupon call or a $100,000 call.

It makes no difference the call type. Following this simple method, I have walked into a customer's home (which was actually a customer issue organization call back) and then walked back out with a happy customer and an additional $100,000 cheque in my hands. How? I listened to the customer's concerns and addressed every one of the concerns honestly and openly. I never missed a single step and built a rapport with the customer as I looked at solutions to solve these concerns. Don't be scared to sell if you're there on a warranty call or a coupon call. I can recall asking my dispatcher once why I was always sent to call-backs and warranty calls. Their response says it all: "Because we have a joke in here that practically every call we send you to, you walk back out with money regardless of the call type."

I have even experienced walking into a coupon call where the previous experience with the organization had not been good. Did I go into a shell and just simply do my tune up and walk away because the customer had a level of hostility there? No. Instead, I discussed the previous issues with the customer, showed empathy and maintained the steps I have outlined in this book. I adapted a few things differently given the unique situation and then, as the call continued, the customer stated how clear and obvious the difference was between myself and other salespeople he had experienced from the organization. You should always strive to set the tone for yourself and set a goalpost for others that work in your business to strive to do the same. From my observations, most sales people out there run calls exactly like the mass-produced, cookie-cutter training teaches and are all too scared to individualize the steps to suit themselves. I cannot emphasize this enough—we are all different and you must find what suits you. Authenticity is key!

Back to my example of the angry customer. By following my approach, my customer ended up purchasing an entire HVAC system from me and was happy about doing so! The customer even reached out to have all of their previous negative reviews removed because he was so pleased and so happy with the experience he received when I took over this situation. All of this was possible because I was upfront and honest, and I was not scared to go after it even though it was a customer issue call.

Remember: It doesn't matter about the nature of the call. Even if it's a warranty call, go after it every time!

CHAPTER 21

EMOTIONAL INFLUENCE

While yes, there are many people who would consider themselves very astute, analytical, and detailed purchasers, they too can be impacted by their emotions when making a purchase. Our emotions drive nearly every decision we make throughout the course of a day. Be it right or wrong, emotions are at the forefront of every decision.

People with certain professional backgrounds will traditionally have a more analytical approach and appear less driven by emotional impulse. Those with an engineering background or who have formal military training may also fit into this type of personality category. On the surface you would say anyone that has been focused on a schedule or routine would tend to analyze the details more than, say, someone that had a less structured approach to their personal or professional life.

Or so you may think . . . I constantly hear from salespeople that it's very difficult to sell anything to this personality type because they will typically pick the price apart and question everything, and that they have no emotion when buying. It is all about the facts and figures. When I was starting out, I also shared this same misconception, especially after listening to what others were saying and thinking it to be true. But when I really looked at each call and thought about the customer after the call was completed, something told me that this surface approach and assumption of this type of customer was not correct. Analyzing each of my past sales interactions, I looked closely at the triggers for customers who were highly analytical (researched products, compared prices and service reviews) and those who were very clearly emotive (driven by feedback from others, very little understanding of product offerings). I then set out to change things up to test different theories I had come up with to gauge the reactions and outcomes of each scenario and optimize my approach. That's right: I actually changed things up and tried new techniques firsthand, and as I have told you many times in this book, decided I would not continue to follow robotic sales tactics that were outdated and didn't feel comfortable and right for me. I decided I would do things my own way, and what I uncovered was that my intuition was right.

It was very apparent to me that, actually, everyone is buying using their emotions whether they want to admit it or not, and whether it is outwardly apparent or not. The person who is openly emotional is also very analytical, but due to their personality you're just not realizing it. You're focused on one facet of their engagement in the sales process and, crazy enough, this is why these are the sales you are losing a high percentage of. These are the customers that I hear about often when talking with others–how the sales call was so easy and the customer was easy to read. They then leave the estimate, and the customers are never heard back from, or if you gained their approval, they cancel prior to work starting.

In this case, you were simply not in control (even though you thought you were!) and allowed the customers' emotions to fool you because you were being lazy with what you perceived was an easy win. And, as a result, you didn't see what was going on right in front of your eyes.

The key is taking the time to understand that different personality types will use different emotions to get to the end result of buying or purchasing. Never assume or treat everyone the same because no one is the same. As I worked on further testing my theory that all purchases are emotive, as I mentioned earlier in this book, I decided I would not put pricing on any option I would present to a customer. I just turned my back on what many even today regard as one of the most important selling tools. I was still a selling technician when I decided to test this theory that I had. I did not care if it was a $100 sale or $15,000 sale, I made the conscious decision that no customer would get to see the price until they had already invested emotionally in the purchase. You need to also build your confidence in testing your own theories on purchase intent. If you fail, you need to see this as still being a positive result, as it has shown you that your theory wasn't correct or that you may still need to refine your thinking further.

Remember: Every problem is just a problem and inevitably has a solution, you just have to spend the time to find it.

Now, removing pricing initially as I did would have most people saying that I am killing my chances at closing the sale. I informed no one of my theory or my undertaking at this time. Yes, this is a big risk, especially if you feel that your sales goals are being closely monitored. But you need to have confidence. It's critical to being able to follow through. I set about doing this and my results simply spoke for themselves. I obviously needed to work harder now developing new skills, those of which I have outlined and shared with you in this book. Of course, customers would ask me what the price is and state they had never experienced a situation where they agreed to buy anything without seeing a price–it's not conventional at all. I simply moved their thought process away from their query about pricing through my response. I acknowledged their query about price, discussing examples how price is only a distraction that can regrettably distort the correct decision, then confidently moved their attention back to the options, guiding them back to carefully reading and choosing–without regret–the one they wanted most of all to feel satisfied.

What you must remember when taking this approach is that you have to be acutely aware of the difference in personalities and how you, in turn, interact with each individual and their unique personality qualities. This revealed to me that my theory was right and that everyone purchases based on emotion.

In observing someone that is analytical, asking a lot of questions and seems to answer after taking time to think rather than off-the-cuff, compared to the person who on the surface seems driven purely by emotion and answers quickly, I discovered that they equally require the same attention to detail to trigger their emotions. Especially the emotions of feeling comfortable, satisfied, and excited to proceed with a purchase.

The difference is the way in which you interact with each of them, in your responses, and in the questions asked and the details in which you want to highlight and make stand out to the customer. Not understanding this is why many salespeople have consistent cancellations and experience what happens when a buyer has remorse. If you want to put an end to this happening, then you need to stop making assumptions about different personality types and stop putting up roadblocks in your own mind before you even give yourself a chance. You need to stop thinking that certain personalities are harder to sell to than others–the only issue is how you perceive them.

I clearly recall being told in a meeting by a so-called "record setting" manager with many years of experience that if you are a person of a certain personality type, it has been proven that it is impossible for you to interact with and gain the trust required to close a sale with other certain personality types. Imagine that! Let's just play that out for a minute. If you can only sell to a certain personality related to your own, you better hope that your customer service team are vetting every call and asking the customer to confirm if they are an extrovert, introvert, analytical purchaser, etc., and if that doesn't happen, well don't bother showing up because the statistical likelihood of you getting an exact personality match to result in a sale are basically zero. As soon as these words of foolish advice were shared, I concluded this manager was not only a fool for believing this but also lazy and unprofessional for not overcoming this obstacle. I can remember, though, the faces of my colleagues and their reactions. They were the opposite of mine, like they had been enlightened, when the truth is they were just given permission to write off each moment of laziness and unprofessional sales behavior as the fault of a mismatched personality. It was an excuse–nothing more, nothing less! The truth is, when I questioned the manager, he couldn't back it up with any scientific proof of his assertation and wasn't too impressed that I'd bothered to question and not blindly accept this information as gospel.

This was reckless to anyone hearing it who was not completely confident in the world of sales. Let's face it, it is human nature to seldom look inward for answers to performance failures. More often than not, salespeople will happily discuss how it was the customers' issue, not theirs. Unless you actually open your mind and change this thought process, you will continue down the path of never being able to increase your revenue. In the weeks following from this training session, as I continued to work hard on learning how to interact with all personality types and not show pricing, this very same manager came to me asking what I was doing differently, given that I had a higher close rate than he had ever experienced. Given the complete arrogance of this person where he was previously gloating about being such an expert, my initial thought was why would I tell him anything? He didn't really deserve it. After all, I had been dismissed when I dared to ask for further explanation regarding his statement around personality types and sales success. I did, however, decide I would give him some insight into what I was doing. Although I certainly didn't spell it out for him, I gave a simple but truthful outline of what I was doing, but I knew that given his arrogance, he would never actually be able to piece it together because that would require him looking inward and questioning himself.

Once I felt that I had solidified my approach and was comfortable not providing the customer with pricing up front, I could see the immediate benefits of my actions. Not only was my close rate and revenue higher but I was running much lower call volumes–working smarter, not harder. On average I was running half the call volume of everyone else in the company. As a salesperson (or a technician) this should be one of your goals, as being able to lower advertising overheads and still earn consistently high revenue is highly attractive to businesses when they look at what an employee brings to the table.

It is important in this topic to again reinforce the importance of giving all calls and all customers the time that they deserve and not rush calls. Taking the appropriate time to truly understand each customer's individual personality type, and to work through any questions and details, is a process step that cannot be underrated and certainly cannot be rushed. You are working towards gaining a customer's trust and for them to purchase using emotion. It takes time to establish that connection where they feel comfortable. If you choose to rush this, you'll end up with a customer experiencing that dreaded buyers' remorse and (likely) cancelling. As you spend the time with the customer authentically listening and discussing solutions, you will now be able to tailor your packages more ideally and pricing will become a much smaller consideration. Their emotive response then becomes one driven by trust and a feeling of being comfortable about what they are being offered, which removes the need to focus on price solely, as the majority of customers will put the value of feeling comfortable with their purchase decision ahead of the cost. The customer is emotionally making a commitment to both you and, most importantly, themselves. The second they make a choice they are emotionally attached, feeling the benefits of their selection.

Once you present your options, which have been structured honestly, and the customer has chosen their preferred option(s), you will then show the customer the pricing for each of the options and have them confirm (again) their preference. More often than not the customer will stay with the original selection they have chosen with positive emotion. Importantly, you have still provided them with all of the information they need and given them the opportunity to make a change if fiscal reasons are also a factor. You must learn how to connect with any and every personality type without fear and be confident that you can connect with positive emotion prior to presenting your options. Failure to achieve this will mean that there is always going to be the chance of negative emotions seeping into the mix when the customer considers an option, which will actually be compounded as soon as they choose one.

Stop fearing personality differences. With the appropriate mindset and willingness to work at building this skill, anyone in sales can achieve the results they are looking for. Remain confident you can close a sale with any personality type. Do not be scared to fail; learn from it and improve. As I became more confident and learned more and more about interacting with different personalities, as I mentioned earlier in this book I decided to delve further into what I had questioned initially, testing the instruction of how your options need to be written with pricing flowing from option-to-option smoothly. It is taught that when a customer reads each option, they will go to a middle-priced option when they see the fiscal increase flows evenly. I would purposely make my options not flow at all, with the pricing ultimately going up and down like a yo-yo, from one to the next. There was seemingly no rhyme or reason in how I positioned each option, although my goal remained to earn profit and revenue from the sale.

There was, however, very much a rhyme and reason to why I was doing this–it would ultimately test the power of every person purchasing purely on emotion. I wanted to see if a person would choose an option without knowing the price, to then see even if it was right beside an option for a substantially lower cost, if this would have any effect at all on their decision.

I have found time and time again that the answer is resoundingly *no*, and that it would not have any impact at all. Even with my options having no flow, it made no material difference to what a customer ultimately chose. Once they made an emotional connection with a particular choice, they did not move away from it.

Remember: Never overlook the fact that all personality types purchase using emotion. Your job is to make sure they purchase using <u>positive</u> emotions.

NOTES

NOTES

CHAPTER 22

VALUING CULTURES IN SALES

We live in a multicultural society, which means you need to understand and respect diverse cultures from around the world.

Not every person from every culture will have the same beliefs regarding sales and sales etiquette as yourself, and this is something you need to understand if you want to broaden your success and be able to cater to the diverse customer base your city may have. This is especially pertinent if you are based in major tech cities such as San Francisco, New York, and Denver. The concept of service-based sales organizations will be quite new for many foreign customers, so as I have covered in this book, don't be scared to educate. Customers appreciate being educated, and this is even more important when dealing with a customer that doesn't have a very clear understanding of the local language. You may need to spend extra time making sure that you convey information that is understood, and sometimes you might even have to ask if there is a family member or someone else that you can talk to as a trusted interpreter and intermediary.

Managing the language barrier within a sales call is critical, as it will determine how effective your call can be and how effective you are in meeting the customer's needs.

Now, you also must understand how different cultures around the world negotiate. There are many cultures where they will not pay the sticker price, nor will they pay the original price listed on any item. There is much respect that comes from negotiating and paying a perceived price lower than the list price. This may seem odd, but to the person this is customary and not something that they are willing to change because they live abroad. These customs are generational and not easily changed, so don't expect that walking into a person's home for 30 minutes will change these beliefs. Don't assume that just because a person moves to your country they have assumed and adopted all of your customs and beliefs. Many will not. I am not saying this with disrespect—I am saying this because these are deeply engrained beliefs. Simply, if you want to get a sale, it's not your place to be offended. If for whatever reason you find you are offended by another person's culture and the way that they interact within a sales call, that raises a completely different potential issue where you need to be true to yourself. If you don't feel that you can honestly give this customer the best service, I would suggest then that you remove yourself from the call and remove yourself from the situation. Potentially speak to the organization you work for and let them know that they need to send out someone else. There is no point staying in that situation if you're not going to sell anything anyway and potentially offend someone, causing a bigger issue for the company.

Over the years I have been approached for advice from co-workers on how to interact with different cultures successfully. In this section I will provide some details of my personal experiences during sales calls for the cultures I have most frequently been asked for advice on.

Remember: Understanding how different cultures like to negotiate is key in this evolving and transient world.

When dealing with people from the Indian culture, for example, they have been taught very early in life on the power of negotiation. Negotiation is seen as a sign of respect and is important in the process of sales. In my experience, when you're putting your options together you need to make sure you do everything per the customers' requirements and use a pricing strategy. When dealing with customers with an Indian background it is a strong approach, and you don't want to put your bottom dollar up first. If you do put your bottom dollar option up first, you will either not get the sale at that price or you will definitely be lowering your price a lot more to get the sale because this customer will not pay the sticker price. You need to make sure that you strategize your options and pricing. You need to adjust your thinking in this scenario. Just because a person wants to negotiate doesn't mean that you need to sell your products and services at a loss—no one expects that. Be prepared when negotiating with this culture, as this sits with you and speaks to the adaptability that I mentioned earlier, which is really an important skill to master to be successful in sales.

Another good strategy aside from just pricing is to load your options up with extra added features if possible. As an example, in HVAC replacement, add in air purification items, hi-tech thermostats, etc.

These are items that customers with this culture will not typically want; however, you're giving yourself more negotiating power later in the call by taking this proactive approach. You should also note when you are building rapport that this is an extremely analytical culture.

Never ask questions you don't know the answer to. Make sure your answers to the customers' questions are complete and do not in any way create new questions. You don't want to give any opportunity for the call to go in a direction you're not ready for. You will need to spend extra time breaking all the issues down and giving financial analysis of the current and future situation around these issues. This customer will base their decision on today's proposed expenditure and the yield of that expenditure (if any) over the next five years. They are not like the majority of your customers that simply look at today's expenditure to solve an immediate issue. This customer looks at every expense as a future investment, so they will be evaluating the costings required today as well as possible future costs that are unknown. They will ask themselves, "If I spend this amount of money today, is it possible that I won't spend anything else and potentially even save money in the next five years?"

The customer will realize and accept that in most cases, the answer is no. You cannot guarantee this, especially when completing a repair. Understand that if you presented options showing items that you expect to last less than five years and the customer has decided to proceed with those today, during negotiating this customer will cleverly turn the costings of those items back at you, as they will be trying to lower the price on the immediate purchase to build a buffer of money to account (with interest) over the next five years to cover the cost of potential replacement in the longer term.

You must always speak directly and plainly when you start negotiating your options and pricing with this customer. Everything you say is analyzed and evaluated quickly, broken down and related to costings specifically. When presenting, you made sure you strategized your pricing and now, you need to sell that price as being better than your standard offering, because if they believe that you have strategized your pricing and have increased it, they won't even negotiate–the deal is over. This customer wants to be sure that they are purchasing at a price lower than their neighbor and anyone else, and unless you allow them to go through this process in a manner that is authentic and respectful, then you are insulting them and their cultural beliefs, which will result in a lost sale. You must not be offended when the customer tells you your price is too high. Instead, remain level-headed and allow the volume of their voice to typically be louder than yours and slow the pace of your responses just a little. By doing this, a very important psychological thing is happening where your customer is feeling in control, which in turn triggers them to relax as they get excited about the savings and good fortune of their negotiation. Now you can begin to discuss pricing in more detail and potentially give a little more in price evaluation from your strategized pricing structure. But don't give too much, as you must fully expect that they will expect a little more. Negotiations are a two-way street and can go back and forward a number of times before settling. When you have hit your pricing strategy basement (your lowest possible price), you may find that the customer will still be asking for "just a little more off the price and we have a deal." It is important at this point to understand and read the customers' body language.

Their body language will tell you if they are telling you the truth and being honest about this statement. It is crucial that you learn how to read the body language of this customer–and really, of any customer that you have. If their body language has not changed from the start of negotiating, they are not telling you the truth and you're still deep in the negotiation. Hold firm and do not be hasty to offer any further reduction right away.

Now remember, in the beginning of this chapter I said you must strategize your options with features that the customer will not want, which will drive up the overall price but gives you additional negotiation space.

When you find yourself in this potential stalemate, it is then time to suggest removing some of these features. This customer will not see this as a loss because they did not want them from the outset. They are focused on the overall price reduction for the base package. However, don't reduce the pricing by the full value of each feature, this way you get back some of the previous price reductions that happened during the initial negotiation. The financial value of this additional reduction is of minor importance compared to previous reductions. It's not what is getting you the sale, it is the self-respect your customer has as they feel they completely controlled the negotiations and successfully drove both the price and package to yield the best possible investment. You have also earned their respect by not shying away from negotiating.

Simply put, to be successful with customers from an Indian background you must learn how to negotiate yourself and learn how to structure your pricing in stages that allow you to flex and maintain your margin goals. I can tell you from personal experience that I have had tremendous success with customers from this cultural background. They absolutely appreciate purchasing at the right price, and as a customer they are extremely loyal, appreciate quality workmanship and if you can financially justify to them an honest-to-goodness package with value for money whilst delivering on everything you've said you would, you will have a customer for life. I have heard from many technicians and top national salespeople over the years that they do not know how to deal with customers who have come from India. This is not an example of the customer winning out, it's the salesperson failing to respect and acknowledge their customers' culture and failing to take the extra time to learn how to do so.

Mutual respect is a very big part of sales and couldn't be truer in this situation. If you don't show respect, you will never get any back. This customer will to a point ignore and generally not listen when they feel they are not being respected, which can be perceived as rude or arrogant, and as a result, many salespeople will not want to run calls with this customer. I have been told many times over the years that respect is not everything. If you believe this statement, then you will have very little success in life. Respect is everything, especially when dealing with a global economy and marketplace who places high social currency on respect. Always remain confident and firm in what you're saying, as this customer will push and challenge you throughout the entire call. When you gain a much more knowledgeable understanding of your customers you will actually start to enjoy working for them and learning about their culture.

Remember: This customer is not trying to be difficult in any way–they are simply acting the way they were generationally taught to purchase.

Another culture that I would like to cover with regards to sales is the Asian culture. I have experienced great loyalty from these customers throughout the years. When on a call or in discussion with a person from this cultural background, you should be very conscious that you must first earn their respect and trust prior to even discussing any pricing. To this customer, respect is extremely important and until it is earned you will not be successful engaging in sales with them. Respect can easily be gained through your demonstration of knowledge and in-depth experience regarding your profession. Also, you must demonstrate very strong self-respect, and by this, I mean don't be afraid to push back a little when the customer makes a statement that you may not necessarily agree with. They will often test this level of self-respect early into the sales call to deem if you are worth spending the time on to discuss possible business dealings. It is an important step in your engagement and demonstrates how important first impressions are with this culture. The salesperson that stands there and simply nods along and agrees is foolish in thinking that this is a successful approach. This customer will test you and will likely start saying things on purpose that contradict your own views or comments. If you have not been authentic and demonstrated proficiency, then you had best pack up and leave because at this moment in time you're showing yourself to have little to no self-respect and this customer will not trust a person who has such little respect in themselves. When you maintain a level head and respectfully hold your position, this customer will give you their respect.

This customer can also be very emotionless in the early stages of your sales call. This is quite normal and should not deter you in any way. Body language will often be difficult to assess with this customer, so it is imperative that you are really focused on addressing the early needs for the establishment of respect. You will be very surprised the first time you are brave enough to go against everything you believe is the preferred way to interact with your customers, and instead of the call going south, it will take a positive direction. You have earned the customers' respect and have demonstrated that you are on their level and are a strong person of character, so now you can really start to focus on the task ahead: the sales call.

When it comes to pricing with this customer, be prepared that you will be expected to enter a level of negotiation. Typically, they will be looking for up to three wins on their part. This can be either through price changes or feature inclusions at no extra cost, as overall product and installation quality is of importance to this customer. So, when you begin building your options you will need to employ some pricing strategy to ensure you end up at the price point and package that still maintains your margins. A potential strategy aside from price changes is temporarily removing an included feature item from your package prior to the presentation.

This customer is not purely driven by price.

Expect to alter the price once or maybe twice at most, and then once approval is initially verbally given, include an item or reintroduce the item you previously removed as a final quality add-on to your package. Alternatively, if you are not at the point yet where verbal approval is given and the customer is pushing for one extra price drop or incentive, another way of ensuring your options are appealing is by including an extended warranty period (if applicable). This customer will generally prefer and appreciate having the extended warranty peace of mind rather than the price drop. Importantly, as you navigate these stages during the negotiation, you need to maintain your level of self-respect, while also maintaining respect towards the customer.

Be ready though: There is one unique final way this culture can choose to negotiate at times, and I will give an example from my own experience.

Once you have approval and start the work, don't be taken aback if the customer comes to you and states that they believe that the work being carried out is not exactly as was agreed. They may try and convince you that you have unintentionally made a mistake and were supposed to do something different, and that now they desire a price reduction because of this perceived error.

It's very important when this happens that you stay level-headed and calm. The customer knows what they are saying is not true and is testing you to see how you will react. This tactic is all about trying to save some more money or to increase the product quality level that you're installing. This is seen as a very pivotal moment for the customer to try this style of negotiation, as you have already begun installing the equipment and are financially obligated to the job itself. The customer is aware that you are financially exposed if you decide to walk away.

This customer will also traditionally manage their payment style to keep this option open. If paying by cash, they will not give you full payment upfront, preferring instead to pay by cheque, knowing they can cancel it. Even if they are financing, this can also be cancelled or paused prior to work completion. They will come to you with the impression of being disappointed that you have in some way disrespected them, even though the opposite is true, in order to test your reaction and response. If everything you did during the call and negotiation stage was not truly what you believed in and was just a weak façade, the customer will know that you will give them what they are asking.

Like me when I first experienced this approach, you may be feeling livid at the audacity of the customer for trying this approach. But, if you don't approach this with absolute resolve and stand by your position, then you open yourself up to conceding or losing the job completely. When this customer witnesses your genuine resolve, they will realize that their attempt at further negotiation is not going to be successful and, in my experience, will likely smile and generally give a statement similar to, "You know, actually, I think you're right. I must have forgot or something." It is at this moment that you have just gained a client for life. You have earned respect and you have given respect. The customer knew all along they were going to try this strategy on you, and you did not get emotional or buckle under pressure. You maintained the original agreement scope AND you just earned their complete unconditional respect. When this customer trusts and respects you, they will always be loyal to you and, of their own accord, will refer you to family and friends with a smile. From my experience I can say that when they call you back for future work, they will never try this strategy again, nor will any of their referrals.

Remember: Respect is of high importance. Without respect, there can be no trust. You must stay committed to your position and package options to maintain self-respect with this culture.

Another culture that I would like to discuss in this book with regards to sales interaction is the European culture. This customer will enjoy a good conversation and be really welcoming into their home, but don't let this fool you. This customer is quite smart when it comes to negotiation. While chatting along with this customer, be aware that their whole aim is to get you feeling really comfortable and hopefully get you to end up talking freely by saying something without actually thinking first. Their aim is to turn the tables back on you, and in doing so they will ask you quite a lot about the pricing expectations of their job, as well as pricing on previous jobs you have completed. Even if you mention to the customer that you can't give pricing just yet, they will still push on this issue, so bear this in mind when you talk to this customer as you are getting your options finalized. You must be very confident in your answers to not give pricing too early in your negotiation. They understand your aims in the sales call, and this customer has the same agenda, which is why they will try very hard to get you to give pricing early on, so that the balance of control is moved in their favor.

However, giving numbers early on opens you up to potential mistakes. These errors come from getting to pricing ahead of your process and having oversight of additional costs. The risk in doing this is that the customer will hold you to those numbers. They will not feel bad knowing that you're doing work below cost. Essentially, their goal is like everyone else's—to try and lower your price as much as possible. Also, be prepared that this customer will actively and frequently look up online what they think is going to be a "fair cost" for materials, or even the total job cost. They may just simply start throwing numbers out to see what reaction they get from you. This is nothing more than a strategy where the customer moves from helping you feel comfortable and welcoming you, to working very hard to get you to feel uncomfortable and rush your responses.

In this situation, stay firm in all your comments and be direct in what you say, as this is what this customer will respect most. As you continue to replicate the reactions and direct answers you not only set the boundaries needed to keep this call successful, but you will also earn that important element of trust and respect. Once you are at the point of creating your proposal, cap your number of options to no more than three. Any more than this and you risk them questioning why there are so many options when they just want the single issue fixed or replaced. This customer will typically not request that you show them anything other than the simplest, most basic repair option. However, don't think for a second you can't gain approval to complete more than the basic option. Instead, you need to have the mindset that with this customer you have to be prepared to build on your options from the basic package and go from there. When you present pricing for your options, the customer will generally ask you for a cash discount even if they have no intention of paying cash. Culturally this is seen as a show of respect, and they will not proceed further in the call if you don't allow them to feel they have received this discount through their negotiation skills. Make sure you strategically position your pricing to allow you to go along with your customer and provide them with a cash price option. In my experience, the customer will pay this price without much more pushing for an additional discount. You just have to be sure your cash price represents a reasonable discount in the customer's eyes.

An additional consideration you should factor into your pricing is to be capable of offering your cash price with financing terms. You are probably shaking your head at this, wondering *what on earth?!* It is a standard request with this customer and one of the final negotiation elements that they will look for in a deal. Even though you should have fully prepared for this in your pricing packages, do not accept it and say yes immediately. You need to push back a little before agreeing to this so the customer can feel a sense of negotiation pride and be happy to purchase.

Remember: Thoroughly know your product and expected pricing as it is represented online for this customer. Be prepared without doubt about your required margins and correct pricing.

CHAPTER 23

INTERACTING WITH SENIORS

I am writing a section here about sales calls involving seniors because I have witnessed many salespeople struggle at various stages during their processes involving seniors. I have also witnessed many seniors upset with the service they have received from previous salespeople.

When running a call for seniors, you must be aware of some small adjustments that you need to make to your style of sales. Senior customers are known for cancelling calls, and this section and advice will help you overcome this and maximize your sales when dealing with this demographic of customer.

It all starts with your tone and approach. Remember, you are talking to someone who is a senior, so do not try and talk at a speed where they don't understand what is needed in order for you to push them to the highest option. I would never condone behavior like this, as this is the behavior of a thief and a scoundrel in my eyes. This customer still may end up wanting to purchase the highest option and often do, but you need to go about it a different way to get there honestly. During this type of call, you will need to slow down and be sure to talk at a speed where your customer can clearly *hear* every word and *understand* every word you are saying. This will mean stopping and checking in with your customer in much shorter increments than you would normally. Be prepared to write things down on paper–if requested–to allow the customer to digest everything at their speed. If you're doing a complete and honest job, you have absolutely no reason to try and rush your customer.

Remember: You will be a senior at some point, and when you are, do you think you're going to lose all the knowledge you have today?

No … so stop treating these customers like they don't know what you're trying to do to them. They can smell a thief a mile off and will simply be polite enough to let you complete your call and then never call you again. Or, if you're pressuring them, they will agree to the job to get you out of their home and leave them alone, then cancel the job within a few hours of you leaving. There is also a fair chance that they will advise their family of their concerns and their family will certainly cancel the work on their behalf. I have seen this happen to salespeople time and again because the salesperson was not authentic and genuine and left the customer feeling intimidated and unheard. Then the salesperson wonders why the call didn't progress, even if they were trying to give a fair deal. Seniors are looking for a high-quality job, as they see very real value in investing in quality products and not having to deal with this issue ever again. Given this purchase need, they generally won't push you over and over to lower your price as long as you have slowed down and taken the time to explain everything to them in ways they understand, and even sat quiet while they read and digest your options or proposal. If you are consistent with this approach with these customers, you will increase your success rate and overall sales ticket.

Remember: Slow down and ensure your customer understands everything regarding product and price beyond any doubt and this customer will stop cancelling.

CHAPTER 24

DEALING WITH THIRD PARTY CUSTOMERS

The topic of landlords is one that makes practically every salesperson cringe in the service industry. My entire approach is based around creating a personal connection, so that you're no longer seen as a salesperson by the customer. In this instance, removing face-to-face contact creates a few extra actions and a unique approach (three phone calls) that I will outline in this section.

First phone call: It is very important that you contact the customer (landlord) over the phone as soon as you arrive at their home. This is how you begin to create the ever-important personal connection. This phone call needs to be made prior to entering the home so that not only can you confirm permission to enter the home, but also set the initial impression and clearly outline with the customer what you're going to be doing in their home. Ask them to tell you the reason that they have made the appointment for you to come to their home on this particular day and the main reason for them booking the call. Explain how you will initially evaluate everything related to their concern, test some things while making notes, and then call them back with an update and possible solutions to solve their concerns and issues. It is very important that you give them an expected time frame in which you will complete this evaluation and to expect your call. When giving them this time frame, also make sure they will be available. If they cannot be available at that time, set a mutually convenient time to reconnect. Prior to ending this phone call, it is really important that you verbally receive their commitment to answering your call when you call back.

Second phone call: Now, after having a brief look over the customer's home and hearing directly from the tenant their own concerns, call the customer back at the agreed time. This is prior to you putting any option considerations together. They will be eager to hear what you have to say, especially if they have not witnessed the issue but are basing everything off the tenant's concerns. Now is the time, especially with landlords, to paint them a worst-case scenario picture and gauge their reaction by how fast they respond, their words and their tone of voice in their response. The reason I am saying to paint a worst-case scenario is because, generally speaking, every landlord is polite and willing to fix anything for a tenant on the surface . . . initially. It is also why the first phone call is so important–it builds some form of rapport so that you're not calling them for the first time with bad news or asking for money. When you call the customer the second time, outline again the steps that you took and then discuss the worst-case scenario example whilst letting them know anything of interest the tenant has also brought to your attention. Be sure they understand this is only an initial review because you have further testing and diagnosis to complete and that you will continue to keep them updated through the process in stages. They will appreciate this approach; however, as reality sets in and they see that they will need to invest money into their home to solve these issues, a landlord will begin to show their true intentions on how willing they are to spend money with you and to what extent. You're not going to miss this cue, as it will be a very honest, emotion-based indicator that they won't be able to hide.

Once you have determined the willingness of the landlord to have any work completed at the home, this is where you now pause the conversation and change direction. Simply remind the customer that currently, you have only been discussing an example of what could potentially be wrong, and the costs associated. Then tell them that now you will complete your diagnosis of their equipment and give them a more comprehensive position. Close out this conversation by advising the customer that you will reconnect with them once you have determined exactly what is needed and how best to proceed. At this point you should pause. You must receive a positive acknowledgment before you say anything else. If you do not receive a positive acknowledgment, you need to build more rapport and rediscuss the reason you are at the home using words similar to those that the landlord used in your initial conversation.

Once you are satisfied more rapport has been built, advise the customer again that you will reconnect once you have determined exactly what is needed to proceed. If the customer is keen to proceed, then you should explain the time frame you are working toward and agree once more on a mutually convenient time to reconnect. I again reiterate how important it is that you have the customer choose the time frame—this way you know they will answer their phone, especially given that they may be feeling anxious about costs. This again is also where your first conversation was really important, as it started to build the feeling of trust and confidence that you need at the forefront of the sales call.

Third phone call: This is where you confidently call the landlord with your confirmed evaluation and finalized options. Because you completed the steps above this conversation will be pleasant. The time between calls is needed to allow the landlord to digest the situation without being pressured. By this point the landlord is viewing you as a trusted professional and will be ready and willing to receive your advice and guidance regarding the option which best suits their needs and home to proceed with.

Following these unique steps when you're sent to a landlord tenant call or discussing options for a potential sale over the phone with a customer will give you the personal connection that you're aiming for with the landlord as well as their full attention and respect to acknowledge everything you're saying. Too often a technician or salesperson will never truly be listened too or acknowledged by a landlord. The requirement for the repair is not as important as it would potentially be if it was in the home that they personally lived in. The communication and work you have put into this call up to this point completing the three strategic phone calls is now your unique point of difference from every other salesperson, and despite the landlord's possible intentions, you have been in control of the entire sales call direction and are now able to drive a successful outcome. The anxiety and annoyance that many salespeople have when they are given a call that deals with a landlord/tenant is unwarranted. There is no need to burn through the call. Many salespeople have convinced themselves that it's not their fault but yes, it is their fault. This is just another call that, with preparation and behaving in a professional manner, can allow you to be successful. It simply requires you to adapt and change a few steps to achieve the same result and win the sale.

Remember: Strategically sequenced phone calls will create a personal connection that will increase conversion on landlord and over-phone service calls.

NOTES

NOTES

NOTES

FINAL THOUGHTS

One of the most important messages I hope you take away from my book is to always remain true to yourself and authentic to your customers. If something doesn't feel right, question it and test it to confirm your own results and answers.

These actions that I have developed, proven, experienced first- hand and shared with you throughout this book will give you the confidence to find the truth within all the noise of sales training. And, more importantly, the confidence to discover your own unique, authentic style in sales.

Throughout this book you will have noted the empty pages. These are intentionally provided for you to use to make notes, jot down your goals and to come back and review as you move forward in your journey. I recommend keeping this handy for days when you may need to refocus or reflect on where you are at. Break down your goals on these pages.

When I first gave thought to writing this book, my inspiration came from being able to really provoke your thoughts and challenge you to improve, evolve and achieve your goals and aspirations. I wanted to really empower readers to respectfully learn to challenge what they are being taught—that the same cookie cutter approach isn't the key to real success. You've got to learn to be a rebel.

Your goal is to not use this as a carbon copy plan to success, but to build your tool kit to take action. To be really focused on understanding and growing your personal sales style and to optimize your potential so that you see the success you deserve for the effort you're willing to put in.

Always enjoy everything you do each day in sales, and as I have shared in this book:

Remember: Nothing at all is impossible, you simply need to find the way to work for and achieve it.

I look forward to hearing about your success.

"You need to make sure your customer trusts you and does feel good about you working on their stuff. Make sure you are the person doing good and treating others good, so people call the company for you."

– PL, 10 years old

www.ingramcontent.com/pod-product-compliance
Lightning Source LLC
Chambersburg PA
CBHW051312220526
45468CB00004B/1309